"I expressed myself in what touched me all my life; in houses, gardens, furniture, ornamentation, and interior design, where imagination, emotion plays."

MADELEINE CASTAING

The World of Madeleine Castaing

RIZZOLI
NEW YORK

New York · Paris · London · Milan

EMILY EVANS EERDMANS
PREFACE BY FRÉDÉRIC CASTAING   FOREWORD BY JACQUES GRANGE

CONTENTS

PREFACE by FRÉDÉRIC CASTAING 7

FOREWORD by JACQUES GRANGE 9

INTRODUCTION by EMILY EVANS EERDMANS 10

IN SEARCH OF LOST TIME 13

LÈVES 39

ACT TWO: MADELEINE THE MERCHANT 78

LE STYLE MALMAISON 133

A UNIVERSE "COCTEAU CASTAING" 167

OF MAISONS MIROIRS 209

EPILOGUE 260

APPENDIX: FABRICS AND CARPETS 263

NOTES 268

BIBLIOGRAPHY 269

INDEX 270

PHOTOGRAPHY CREDITS 271

ACKNOWLEDGMENTS 272

PREFACE

There's a cardboard box covered in blue fabric. Inside, some family papers: baptismal certificates, birth certificates, marriage certificates, family register. . . . Some yellowed photos, too: my grandfather and my grandmother in Paris or at Lèves with Satie, Picasso, Cocteau, Soutine, Cendrars, Malraux; my father on horseback in front of the house or in his First Communion suit at the foot of the double staircase; my sister and I playing on the terrace . . . . And several newspaper clippings, one in particular: my grandmother responding to a journalist . . . .

Making a house is creating. I make houses like others write poetry, make music, or paint. A house is more of a likeness than a portrait. Don't be intimidated by audacity; be audacious, but with taste. You also need intuition, originality, vigor. Avoid reproduction, that easy and banal method. Don't get taken in by fashion. A secret: love your house; love makes miracles.

The shop on rue Jacob wasn't anything like those antique shops with exceptional furniture lined up in paradelike fashion. It was more of a real house with a fire going in the fireplace, elegant yet familiar furniture, lamps everywhere, real bookshelves with real dog-eared books. English tables, a Chinese screen, Neoclassical objects, Russian armchairs, statues, paintings by Soutine, photos of Baudelaire, of Hugo, and of the grandchildren—in this way an entire network of bonds, affinities, harmonies, and secret correspondences was created.

Lèves was the family house. The memory of Soutine, who died during the war, was ever-present. In the garden near the little ivy-covered fountain where we played as kids he had painted "the woman with her feet in the water." In the house, we listened wide-eyed while my grandfather told us how the mysterious Soutine would get up in the middle of the night and leave his room, knife in hand, to slash his paintings.

One day when we were about eight or ten years old, my brother and I took all of the household silver and buried it near the water, like in *Treasure Island*. We made a map, established landmarks.

The treasure has never been found.—**FRÉDÉRIC CASTAING**

A young Frédéric Castaing sitting with his grandmother in the dining room at Lèves.

FOREWORD

There exist magical places.

Lèves, near Chartres, with its Neoclassical extravagance, is one of them. Madeleine Castaing's masterpiece, in a unique and personal style inspired by early nineteenth-century houses and literature, is timeless. That century, which she considered full of artistic wealth, was her source. (She said that Balzac and Stendhal were unequaled decorators.) Madeleine was extremely cultivated and she had the skill to be able to start out as a decorator at Lèves. It was such an accomplishment that she devoted herself to decorating in the boutique that she opened in 1946 on rue Jacob. It was an immediate success.

She looked at things not as a decorator, but as an artist. Before her, a house and a garden had never been created in harmony; she considered them as one. At a time when houses were sad, she introduced poetry, a taste for life, and mystery. "There is always beauty in mystery," she said.

She surprised and surprises still. She makes us feel emotions that, before her, we didn't know existed in interior design. She created a perfect balance between decoration, architecture, and landscape. The lush atmosphere at Lèves, with its ivy-eaten sculpture and its cinematographic and literary mise en scène, gives the feeling of an extremely weightless coincidence.

I met Madeleine Castaing in 1969. I already admired her work and from that point on, I loved her, too. She was like her décors. An enchantress. Vivacious, happy, sensual, free, intelligent, friendly, and exceptionally young at heart. Her world buzzed with anecdotes about Satie, Picasso, Cendrars, Modigliani, Soutine, and Maurice Sachs, all of the greats with whom she shared so many passions.

Madeleine had three reasons for living: The first, the leitmotif of her life, to love and be loved by her husband Marcellin. Then comes Soutine, whom she considered to be the greatest painter of the century. And in far last was that brilliant and worldwide success about which she would say, "I make houses like others write poems," what would become known as *le style* Madeleine Castaing. Inimitable.—**JACQUES GRANGE**

Legendary designer Jacques Grange pays homage to his mentor Madeleine Castaing in this effortlessly elegant dining room. Neoclassical furniture and Regency striped pink walls are masterfully matched with Madeleine's Empire style "Carrelage Castaing" carpet.

INTRODUCTION

Muse, Magician, Maecenas, Merchant, Mythmaker — all have been used to describe Madeleine Castaing whose compelling style continues to beguile and mesmerize to this day. Reader, dreamer, traveler, bargainer — and even though she considered the following distasteful — decorator, can all be added to the list as well. During the nearly ten decades of her life, she assumed all these roles in full and played them to the hilt.

To enter the world of Madeleine Castaing—a world carefully constructed out of romantic novels and nineteenth-century props—is to enter a stream-of-consciousness in which it is unclear what is reality and what is a dream. To document and catalogue her career and the creation of *le style* Castaing is, in many instances, like trying to gather sand. Castaing herself purposely told conflicting accounts of the same events—continually reshaping them until they matched her poetic vision of her past, and other than the memories of her intimates and colleagues, left no archives. What we are left with then is the story of Castaing as she wished it to be—and for a book about her style which is inextricably linked with her imagination—perhaps this is exactly how it should be.

Why does Castaing style continue to fascinate? If Madeleine were here to answer that question, she might reply, "It's all about life." While many may smile when they describe the stuffing coming out of a chair or some other example of extreme wear and tear found in so many of her rooms, it was precisely these imperfections and traces of its inhabitants—real or out of a nineteenth-century novel—that breathed life into her spaces and gave them soul. When a client despondently told her that her dog had made a stain on the carpet, Madeleine's response was "Excellent!" and she meant it.

A key characteristic of Madeleine's work that places it firmly in the annals of design history was her purposeful disregard for convention. It may be difficult for our eyes today to see how rebellious many of Madeleine's choices were at the time, but her peers certainly stopped in their tracks and, before long, copied. She launched the fashion in France for English Regency furniture after World War II and peppered her rooms with Napoleon III, the absolute epitome of bad taste at the time. She was the first to merchandise her shop as if it were a private residence, and even developed her own line of fabrics which, in France, could only be purchased directly from her. With no training or a mentor, Madeleine was fearless and confident, never doubting her gut or her eye. (These traits were shared by another legendary lady of style and near contemporary, Coco Chanel, who also found success by doing it her way.)

If she preferred living in a setting that recalled the past, it shouldn't be inferred that she took a passive approach to living itself. On the contrary, she was a shrewd businesswoman, who would bargain to the last centime, and a brilliant marketer who knew how to sell her flea-market finds for 1000 times their value. Not that her clients complained—they weren't buying the object as an investment, rather it was as a talisman of her universe that it held its value.

The story—or rather, many stories—of Madeleine Castaing at times reads like romantic fiction and at others takes us through many turbulent and enthralling moments in twentieth-century history. From a young bourgeois schoolgirl who left convent life for the arms of her one true love, to the electric art scene of Paris in the '20s where she and her husband hobnobbed with Picasso and Modigliani, to opening her own shop in the full-throttle of World War II on the verge of turning fifty—this was a woman with an appetite for life, and a talent for making it suit up to her own demands.—**EMILY EVANS EERDMANS**

Madeleine striding down the boulevard in the south of France full of the purpose and confidence that allowed her to always follow her heart.

IN SEARCH OF LOST TIME

"'I'll invent my life,'
Julietta had said to her mother upon
announcing her engagement."

LOUISE DE VILMORIN, *Julietta* (1953)

On December 19, 1894, the very day Captain Alfred Dreyfus's court-martial for treason commenced, Madeleine Castaing began her life as Marie Madeleine Marielle Magistry in Chartres, France. A child of the haute bourgeoisie, she was born into comfortable circumstances, enjoying a protected and privileged upbringing even while political scandal threw the French Republic into turmoil. Her father Auguste was an engineer commissioned at the time by the city to update its train station. Her mother Noëlie, "a ravishing woman, full of charm, an extraordinary charm, and very sophisticated,"[1] had grown up nearby and for the duration of Madeleine's childhood, the Magistrys divided their time between Madeleine's maternal grandparents' property, the Villa des Roses, in Saint-Prest, and a *hôtel particulier* on the rue La Bruyère in Paris.

The Villa des Roses, which Madeleine compared to Marcel Proust's Combray, would serve as one of her earliest and most compelling influences. The house ignited her love of houses from the young age of eight[2] and evoked potent memories decades later: "The black furniture, the glass of absinthe, my grandfather's white cardigan, a dense garden, more Combray than Combray itself, that went all the way down to a branch of the Eure River."[3]

Her mother's bedroom in particular made a vivid impression on her: "It was hung in pink fabric and above there was muslin with big balls of white cotton . . . ."[4] Noëlie's father, the magnetic Rodolphe Burgues, who had founded the political newspaper *La Presse* and helped launch France's first news agency, presided over the Villa. The constant flow of lively and cultivated conversation from Rodolphe's distinguished guests later permeated Madeleine's own salons, whether at her country house in Lèves or fireside in the middle of her Paris shop.

Madeleine ("Marie" was much too prosaic a name and soon abandoned as noted by her biographer Jean-Noël Liaut) was the oldest of Auguste and Noëlie's children. She was followed by brothers Roger, Gérard, and finally Pierre who was conceived out of an extra-marital affair of Noëlie's. Like her grandmother and mother before her, she was sent to board at the convent school

Madeleine and Marcellin strolling in the Midi. Madeleine regarded their marriage, which spanned over forty years, her greatest life's work. The story of their whirlwind romance, as told by Madeleine, inspired Louise de Vilmorin to write the novella *Julietta*.

Madeleine's favorite author Marcel Proust wrote evocatively of his Aunt Leonie's house in Illiers-Combray. To the left of the bed sits a madeleine, which Proust famously described in *À La Recherche du temps perdu*.

The traditional decoration of Aunt Leonie's dining room was typical of the Third Republic and very much like Madeleine's grandparents' house, Saint-Prest, which she called more "Combray than Combray."

Les Dames Blanches du Sacré Coeur in Chartres with the children of the local leading families. While Madeleine didn't excel at her studies, she whiled away many hours in the pages of books, favoring the romantic novels of Chateaubriand, Stendhal, and Balzac. A passage from Balzac's *Le Lys dans la vallée*, a tale of unrequited love and one Madeleine read several times, perfectly exemplifies the literature that stoked the starry-eyed schoolgirl's amorous fantasies:

> Love has its blazon, and the countess discerned it inwardly. She gave me a poignant glance which was like the cry of a soldier when his wound is touched; she was humbled but enraptured too. My reward was in that glance; to refresh her heart, to have given her comfort, what encouragement for me!

Her lifelong passion for literature and her ability to disappear into fictional places and times began here.

Madeleine's lasting interest in her sartorial style was apparent from a young age. Laure Lombardini, Madeleine's long-time assistant, who also attended the same convent, remembers, "she … often said to me that her uniform was the height of chic. It was a fluted hat, a white veil of very fine wool muslin, a dress made of the same material with the Heart of Jesus and Mary embroidered on it, and a black overcoat. And she wore low-heeled oxfords."[5] It was also at this time, Madeleine claimed, that she first made the acquaintance of one of her enduring loves: a house in Lèves, a small town just a few kilometers to the north of Chartres.

> Lèves … it was a wonderful house. When I discovered it, I had just turned 13; I was living with the Visitandines [*sic*] in Chartres, a convent with never-ending stark, white hallways. On Thursdays, we would go take a walk in the surrounding countryside. And there was a part of the landscape there that fascinated me: part of a path, a little bridge over a waterfall and a big crumbling wall. What was behind that wall? I was haunted by a mystery that I imagined to be captivating.[6]

No doubt, the romantic ruins behind the wall completed the spell of enchantment cast over her. There stood a Directoire manor house, once the summer residence of the bishops of Chartres, abandoned and in disrepair. Only a few years later she met her other great love, whom she soon convinced to make the house hers.

Several versions abound on how Madeleine met Marcellin Castaing at the age of fifteen. The dramatic tale was most likely embellished and polished over time by Madeleine and certainly it compared to any first encounter depicted in the novels she devoured, so much so that it ultimately inspired its own novelette, *Julietta*, by Madeleine's friend Louise de Vilmorin.

The most likely course of events, according to Liaut, is as follows: While en route by train to the spa town of Cauterets in the Pyrenees with her mother Noëlie, Madeleine noticed a man on the street in Toulouse and then again at the train station. She later described Marcellin: "He was exactly my type of man. He was tall, blond, dark blond, blue eyes, very blue. I thought he was handsome."[7]

Madeleine and Marcellin strolling through the Place Stanislas in Nancy as a young couple before they moved to Paris and became part of its exhilarating art scene. Madeleine's love for dramatic hats was a lifelong affair.

Vallée-aux-Loups, the country house of François-René de Chateaubriand, was reinterpreted back to the writer's time in 1967. The flora-and-fauna patterned carpet and trellis-overlaid walls in the entrance hall would certainly have met with Madeleine's approval.

One of the two salons at Vallée-aux-Loups whose décor evokes the romantic atmosphere of a charterhouse. Chateaubriand's immediate connection to this "gardener's house, hidden among forest-covered hills" in 1807 is reminiscent of Madeleine's to Lèves.

Between 1830 and 1837, Balzac retreated to his friend Jean de Margonne's Château de Saché. Here he wrote Madeleine's beloved *Le Lys dans la vallée*, which was based on Saché and the other chateaux in the Indre-et-Loire area. The trompe l'oeil wallpaper in the grand salon dates back to 1803.

The dining room at the Château de Saché is a vibrant blue and retains its original classical frieze from 1825. When in residence, Honoré de Balzac would nap after dinner until midnight and then write until morning, sustained by large amounts of coffee.

Back on the train, she realized he was sitting in the neighboring compartment. While her mother napped, Madeleine decided to go to this mysterious and handsome stranger and declare herself. The man was so taken by this young girl's avowal that he proposed they get off the train together at the next stop. Panicked by this suggestion, she refused, only to agree hours later. After their liaison, the man returned Madeleine to her mother and their engagement was presumably agreed upon.

Regardless of precisely how their first encounter transpired, Madeleine's behavior was as daring as any of the heroines in her novels: If they hadn't become betrothed, Madeleine's future prospects of marriage would have been ruined and it was for marriage that Madeleine and her contemporaries were groomed. Five years later in 1915, Madeleine married Marcellin Castaing, unlikely dressed, according to Madeleine "in a Greek dress with my bare feet in sandals" at Saint-Prest.

Marcellin, born in 1880, was fifteen years older and many inches taller than the petite Madeleine. (Historically, most accounts have cited Marcellin as over twenty years older than Madeleine. Perhaps this inaccuracy was encouraged by Madeleine who may have wished to appear younger or merely thought a wider age difference was more dramatic and romantic.) He hailed from a wealthy Toulousian family with extensive property holdings, including vineyards. When he met Madeleine, Marcellin was the mayor of the small town of Longages and intent on pursuing a political career. When World War I broke out soon after their nuptials, Marcellin was working for the prefecture in Nancy. It was a trying period for Madeleine: In addition to the tedium of her daily routine, she lost her brother Roger to the war and her mother, whom she adored, to illness.

Once again, it was to books she turned for escape and solace, including *Du côté de chez Swann*, the first of Marcel Proust's seven volume semi-autobiographical novel *À La Recherche du temps perdu*. Madeleine claimed to have read this 3000-page modern masterpiece an astounding twelve times and often cited it as one of her main influences. Her favorite lament was to bemoan how Proust had died two days before she was arranged to meet him: "It was the biggest disappointment of my life."[8] Recounted in a stream-of-consciousness manner, the novel places primary emphasis on memory, and weaves the past and present in and out of each other so intricately that the distinct boundaries of each disappear. Madeleine was far from apologetic about her love of the past. Not only did she admit that the unfashionable nineteenth-century style of her childhood was in effect the basis of her style, she also once commented "… nostalgia isn't so bad, it allows you to express things which come from the heart."[9]

Being contained in the provinces did not appeal to Madeleine, and after giving birth to her two sons, Michel in 1918 and Bernard the following year, she was determined to convince Marcellin to put his political career aside so that they could leave the dull waters of the provinces for the glittery lights of Paris. Madeleine may have been a dreamer and a creator of her own reality that was more

A wax figure of Marcel Proust in his favorite position, reclining in bed, at the Château de Breteuil, which appeared in Proust's *À La Recherche du temps perdu* as Bréauté. Hannibal de Bréauté, based on the chateau's proprietor Henri de Breteuil, was described as one who "mixed with no one below the rank of Highness. But he laughed at them in his heart and longed only to spend his days in museums."

in keeping with her romantic reveries than the cold, hard facts, but she also had an iron will and when she was intent on achieving or acquiring something, she got it. Marcellin knew this better than anyone, and to Paris they went, where he traded in politics for art and literature.

ASCENDING MONTPARNASSE

"Oh how does everything begin everything comes undone and everything starts again
I remember Montparnasse in the first days of autumn
You order a café crème and people are less amazed to see us
Than we ourselves to be together with the future ahead of us."

LOUIS ARAGON, *Il ne m'est Paris que d'Elsa* (1964)

Paris in the 1920s was a sumptuous feast where talent, ideas, and a furious desire to live every moment to the fullest were in abundance. Poets and artists from all points were drawn like moths to a flame. The epicenter of this creative mecca where studios were affordable and cheap red wine flowed as freely as paint and ink was the Left Bank neighborhood of Montparnasse.

Having moved to Paris after the end of World War I, Marcellin and Madeleine lost no time in soaking up the city's diverse offerings. Although they took up residence on the rue Victorien-Sardou in the well-heeled and buttoned-up residential 16th arrondissement, Marcellin's new position on the staff of *Floréal*, a cultural review of art, literature, and theater, thrust the Castaings into the heart of Paris's exhilarating art scene.

A daily line-up of exhibitions, lectures, and balls made for a fervent and dizzying schedule—the better to forget the revulsions and losses of war. Long nights of champagne, dancing, and frivolity numbed the disillusionment of a generation made wiser by the ravages of global conflict. With a nurse to look after her young sons, Madeleine had nothing to hold her back. "I loved my kids until they were three years old,"[10] she joked to a friend, but in truth neither Madeleine nor Marcellin had strong parental instincts and their two sons Bernard and Michel grew up in a world of boarding schools and governesses. It goes without saying that Marcellin's miniscule salary as a writer far

Luxurious foliage encircle Madeleine and her first son Michel who was still young enough here to keep his mother amused. It wasn't long after that she embraced the heady social swirl of Montparnasse.

from covered the Castaings' lifestyle of cook, chauffeur, couture, private schools, paintings, parties, and addresses in both town and country. A generous subsidy from his family allowed Marcellin and Madeleine to dedicate themselves fully to living *la vie* Montparnasse.

Most every evening found the couple holding court at the café La Rotonde where Marcellin kept an open table. La Rotonde, situated on the sunny side of the Carrefour Vavin at the intersection of the boulevards Montparnasse and Raspail, was the stomping ground of many artists and writers. The generous policies of proprietor Victor Libion did much to attract his often cash-strapped clients. La Rotonde was the only café in the neighborhood where one could stay for hours without reordering; where the croissants and baguettes weren't watched with a hawkish eye; and where bills could be settled with a drawing or a painting. Here luminaries past, present, and future gathered for drink and conviviality: Modigliani, Matisse, Chagall, and Braque all were weaving in and out of tables at the ultimate cocktail party. Madeleine described the moment:

> It was interesting to witness the whole movement. Everyone was in Paris. Every language could be heard, and in the evening all the painters were at Montparnasse. What fascinated me was that I caught sight of Trotsky, Lenin, and the big Derain strutting around, too. Picasso, no, never. He didn't go down to Montparnasse much. He stayed in Montmartre.[11]

The Castaings—who had a natural interest in contemporary art—had started collecting early in their marriage. While taking an evening stroll in Toulouse, they came upon students hurling stones at a gallery window. "We went up to the window and saw a painting that stopped us in our tracks. It was a nude by Modigliani. We went in, looked at it, and were completely taken with it. We stayed there in front of that painting for an hour and bought it."[12] There is no doubt that collecting for Madeleine was an intense experience where a visceral connection to the work was primary. If she was struck by a work, she took decisive action: "If I saw a painting I liked at an exhibition, I'd buy it. I bought a really pretty picture by Matisse that had a pink scarf in it, and a big nude by Modigliani. It was superb. I also bought Utrillo and Rouault."[13] Looking at pictures, meeting artists, and encouraging them with support—financial and otherwise—was an activity the couple savored and which brought them together.

The Paris art market of the 1920s was at a pumped-up high. Speculation and conspicuous consumption drove prices to a premium, and visits to artists' studios were part of the social whirl. Due in no small part to Jean Cocteau, the gap between high society and Montparnasse's avant-garde had been bridged during the war and the two mingled seamlessly, each adding glamour and novelty to the other. Cocteau, whose energy was matched only by his ambition, made a conquest of Picasso, the magnetic center of the Parisian art world. Laid low by the death of his companion Eva Gouel and war fatigue, Picasso was more than ever susceptible to the charms of "The Frivolous Prince," who

Opposite: This portrait of a chicly bobbed Madeleine with Cupid's bow lips bears out poet and auteur Blaise Cendrars's desire to make her the Mary Pickford of France; Following: A typical night of revelry at the café La Rotonde where Madeleine and Marcellin kept an open table and hobnobbed with Modigliani, Soutine, and other art world notables.

had already established himself as the darling of the highly exclusive and fashionable set of Charles and Marie-Laure de Noailles.

Maurice Sachs, a frequent visitor to Lèves, recounted in *Le Sabbat*:

Neither Apollinaire, Max Jacob nor Picasso greeted the arrival of the salon poet with any enthusiasm. But what had initially appeared a conflict of interests proved skin-deep . . . . Cocteau was given the key to a new idiom . . . introduced to the secret held by those hardened, poverty-stricken artists, who were in truth both greater men and poets than he, and allowed to partake of their shared discoveries provided he employed his marvelous gifts of communication to popularize and promote the hidden treasure which, after all, someone had to exploit so that the community may live . . . .[14]

Picasso went against the grain of high art when he agreed to design the sets and costumes for the new ballet *Parade*, with libretto by Cocteau, choreography by Léonide Massine which would be performed by Serge Diaghilev's Ballets Russes, and music by Erik Satie. "Mr. Renan never scandalized the Sorbonne as much as Picasso did the café La Rotonde when he accepted my proposition," quipped Cocteau. Its spring 1917 premiere brought habitués of boiseried salons together with the art world's elite and represented a revolutionary new order where fashion and wealth were cheek by jowl with the avant-garde. Years later, Madeleine remembered herself in the center of the scene: "I went to the premiere where people threw umbrellas, bags, everything! Hats were flying, yelling erupted from everywhere . . . . I saw [Satie] backstage raising up his hands and shrugging his shoulders at all the noise."[15] However, as *Parade* opened during the height of the war while the Castaings were still living in Nancy, this experience most likely took place in Madeleine's imagination, rather than in reality.

Madeleine, however, did befriend Erik Satie, the bohemian composer of *Gymnopédies* (which Madeleine wished to have played at her funeral). The scandal of *Parade*—whose orchestrations included parts for a typewriter, lottery wheel, and pistol—put Satie's name on the map at the age of fifty-one. Madeleine undoubtedly was fascinated by this eccentric and original personality. Possessed of a wonderful humor he composed *Trois Morceaux en forme de poire* in response to the criticism that his work had no form. He lived in a dingy one-room apartment in the working-class suburb of Arcueil to which he would allow no visitors, yet he was always fastidiously turned out in a bowler hat and grey velvet suit. One thing that can be said of Madeleine was that there was no snobbery when it came to her friends. Wit, an interest in literature and painting, and a streak of individualism were more compelling to her than a blueblood background or proper comportment. Several of her intimates, such as Maurice Sachs, were notorious for their *mal élevé* behavior, but Madeleine's tolerance was inexhaustible to the extent one might think she was amused by displays of insolence.

Another acquaintance Madeleine made at La Rotonde was that of Swiss novelist and poet Blaise Cendrars who, during his turn as a film impresario, was intent on making Madeleine "the

The composer Erik Satie with Madeleine and a young Michel walking the grounds of Lèves in 1923. Satie earned the nickname "The Velvet Gentleman" from his daily uniform of identical grey velvet suits of which he seemed to have an inexhaustible supply.

Mary Pickford of France." Cendrars was one of the first members of the French avant-garde to be a passionate proponent of cinema. He once said "truth is imaginary" and perhaps it was his example of reshaping his past that inspired Madeleine to mold her own memories to her liking. Born Frédéric Louis Sauser, he created the name "Blaise Cendrars" from "*braise*" (embers) and "*cendres*" (ashes) with "*ars*" (art) added to the mix.

Cendrars lived as though addicted to adventure and novelty. By the time his path crossed with Madeleine's in 1922, he had traveled on at least three continents, witnessed the Russian Revolution, fought in World War I during which he lost part of his right arm, and was driving around in an Alfa Romeo color-customized by Georges Braque. The American writer Henry Miller, his friend in later years, described him as a man "exploding in all directions at once."

Cendrars made his first foray into film while assisting the director Abel Gance on the 1919 film *J'accuse!* After Madeleine's screen test confirmed her looks translated onto film, Cendrars proposed he adopt one of the acclaimed classics of French literature as a star-making vehicle for the both of them. For the next few years, they searched for the right project: *Madame Bovary* held the promise of being a role which Madeleine could feel close to and lose herself in, which Cendrars wrote was key to overcoming "the major difficulty" that is "acting, meaning the expression, the dramatic intensity, the embodiment of a character that isn't you."[16] After failing to obtain the rights from Gustave Flaubert's niece, the project fizzled. Years later, Madeleine bemusedly remembered the conclusion of her venture at movie stardom: "Cendrars thought of *Maria Chapdelaine* [a 1913 novel by Louis Hémon on French-Canadian pioneer life]. I was afraid of being cold and I said no. And that was it for me and the movies."

It wasn't long before the Castaings made the acquaintance of the painter who would become the concentrated focus of their collecting and whose work could be ranked as Madeleine's third passion, after Marcellin and Lèves: Chaim Soutine. While at La Rotonde with their friend the painter Pierre Brune, the Castaings remarked on a savage-looking, brooding man. Brune explained that it was a struggling artist whom they should help by buying a picture. Another version was recounted by Madeleine in the 1970s in which Brune first mentioned Soutine at her home in the 16th arrondissement, rather than at La Rotonde; as the less dramatic sequence of events, it rings truer. In any case, the Castaings agreed and an appointment was planned.

> We arrived at a little bistro on the rue Campagne-Premiere at 8:00. It was behind a coal merchant's store. No light. Eight o'clock, 8:15, we had a dinner to go to. Eight twenty. Finally, Soutine arrives with two big paintings. We couldn't see anything. Marcellin takes 100 francs and says to him, "What I want is to see those paintings. We'll go tomorrow or the day after tomorrow to your studio. Either way here's 100 francs tonight as an advance for what I buy from you." Soutine takes the bill, throws it at my husband's feet, takes the paintings, and leaves. "You could've given me five francs [his standard fee]," he said, "and taken my painting, and I would have been the happiest man alive."[17]

(At the end of her life, Madeleine told another tale of the meeting and admitted that it was she and Marcellin who were late and in a hurry. As her biographer Jean-Noël Liaut concludes, "How do you find your way out of such a maze? Which version do you keep? Questions that will never have an answer; any Cartesian approach completely eludes Madeleine's uncontrollable imagination."[18])

Years later, the Castaings were stopped in their tracks by a still-life painting of a chicken suspended over a plateau of tomatoes, which they were grieved to discover wasn't for sale. So insistent were the collectors that Soutine's dealer Leopold Zborowski pressed its owner Francis Carco to part with it.[19] Madeleine scoured Paris for other pictures by the same artist and finally found, for 800 francs, a portrait of an old woman "with pink skin, white hair, frizzy and thin, white hands covered with blue veins, done-up for the portrait, but strained from being both shy and proud of being painted . . . . That was it. We were won over, my husband and I, and we consistently had but one goal: to buy Soutines."[20]

Chaim Soutine was born in 1893, a year before Madeleine, but into circumstances far removed from Madeleine's privileged bourgeois cocoon. He was raised in a Jewish shtetl in Lithuania within an orthodox family of limited means, and bore witness during his childhood to devastating pogroms and poverty. These experiences haunted Soutine whose work served as an outlet for his rage and anguish in his work. Without support from his family to pursue his artistic inclinations, he left home to study drawing at the Fine Arts Schools in Minsk and Vilnius. By 1913, he was in Paris and found his way to La Ruche, an artists' colony located in the Passage Dantzig where many Eastern Europeans congregated. It was most likely here that Soutine and the Italian-Jewish artist Amedeo Modigliani first met.

An unlikely friendship was struck up between Modigliani and Soutine. The former possessed a warm, lively temperament reflective of his Mediterranean background which made a strong contrast to the shy and gruff Soutine whose rudeness and savagery have become fabled. Together they consoled themselves in long nights of carousing and imbibing wine, absinthe, and cocaine (a toxic cocktail which ultimately ruined Soutine's stomach). Modigliani and Soutine were both habitués of La Rotonde—where a few pictures of the former hung on the wall as payment for his many hours there—and Madeleine recalled seeing Soutine there, "a character out of a Dostoyevsky novel,"[21] glancing over at their table. But it was not Soutine's style—far from it—to table hop and chat up possible collectors.

The two shared a studio together and Modigliani, who fervently believed in his friend's work, convinced his dealer Zborowksi to take him on. After Modigliani's untimely death in 1920 which profoundly affected his friend, Soutine painted furiously, producing hundreds of canvases in a matter of months. Although "Zbo" reluctantly did take on the surly Lithuanian—paying Soutine a meager five francs per canvas—his efforts were well-rewarded when the sale of Soutine's entire

output to the American millionaire Dr. Albert C. Barnes in 1922 enabled the dealer to open his own brick-and-mortar premises at 26, rue de Seine. Soon Soutine was seen elegantly attired in a suit and fedora suggesting that his reputation for slovenliness had more to do with his penury rather than an inherent uncivilized disposition. He read Balzac and Zola, took lessons to lose his Yiddish accent and preferred to court the coiffed mannequins of the fashion houses, even if they mocked him, rather than to warm himself in the ready embraces of prostitutes.

In 1925, when Zborowski heard that the Castaings were on the hunt for Soutines, he offered them *Garçon de choeur* for the costly sum of 30,000 francs. The painting became their third Soutine, although Madeleine often liked to claim it was their first as it was the picture she was "most passionate about." It was a decisive moment: "After that we decided to sell off all our collection and devote ourselves entirely to collecting Soutine's. This was partly because Soutine's were so expensive—30,000 francs each, a very high price at the time—but mainly because we agreed with the critic Elie Faure . . . that Soutine was the greatest painter of the period."[22]

Upon renewing their acquaintance with the artist, Madeleine and Marcellin believed Soutine to be a genius and thought his work more important than any of his contemporaries. If their first meeting was a disaster, Soutine was mollified and even avenged by the Castaings' fervid interest in his work. And so, as Madeleine recounted in 1939, ". . . a real-life adventure begins that's still going on—a fabulous adventure in which the most contradictory feelings were expressed and overcome by our absolute faith in his genius."[23]

It is interesting to note that even before they made the decision to focus solely on Soutine, the Castaings' taste in collecting didn't include the fashionable contemporary movements of Cubism and Surrealism. To then dedicate their resources to a single painter and one who stood outside the firmament speaks to the Castaings' confidence not only in Soutine, but in their own eye. Although Soutine's work, by virtue of its virulent colors and dynamic brushwork, is often labeled Expressionist, it wasn't self-consciously so as Soutine took no heed of stylistic innovations. Rather he reverentially looked to the work of old masters, especially Rembrandt, in developing his painterly style. If there is a brutality to his work, there is also a stylish elegance, both of which would have appealed greatly to Madeleine.

Madeleine saw Soutine as the heir to Vincent van Gogh. She decreed in an interview given in the last year of her life: "As with van Gogh, there will be a reassessment of his painting and he will be known as the painter who lit up the twentieth century."[24] The vigor with which he worked was matched by his precise working conditions: He used only seventeenth-century canvases because they were smooth enough to not drag his brush; he kept his palette remarkably pristine; and his pigments had to be ordered from overseas. Yet even when these conditions were met, Soutine more

After Marcellin's death, Madeleine brought many of her favorite Soutines to her Paris apartment, including *Baigneuse*. It was painted around 1931 during the period Soutine was a frequent visitor to Lèves.

often than not found fault with his work and the majority were burned or cut up into pieces. Dealers famously hid his work or hung it out of reach so that Soutine wouldn't have access to destroy it.

Perhaps after years of wandering and poverty, what Soutine most craved was security and he finally found it in the Castaings, who gave him a refuge at their country house in Lèves and a guarantee of a home for his work. "In our company he became more sociable,"[25] Madeleine said and, during the 1930s, his painting became more subdued in color, theme, and brushwork leading some to conclude that he had finally found some respite from his demons and many others to announce that in this mature phase Soutine became a master.

Madeleine first posed for Soutine in 1929 and at least three known portraits of her are known. She recalled one of the sittings for which he was invited to Lèves:

> It was springtime. The weather was nice so that we were already staying in the countryside. The driver was supposed to take me into town to Soutine's studio and wait for me. And one night—it was incredible, in fact—I posed for a lot of painters, but never . . . I posed for Beran, for Brune. I posed for Kremègne, for Favory. But you can't imagine what it was like to pose for Soutine. He almost raped his models. He stayed in front of me; it could get dark and he'd still be painting. He was in such a state! When he was done, he was despondent from fatigue and emotion. One night, he didn't want to let me go. I said to him, "Come on. They're waiting for me at home. It's dinnertime." He said, "I'm coming with you." That's how he came to our countryside house.[26]
>
> . . . He admired our house and garden so much that Marcellin suddenly had an idea: "Soutine if this place inspires you then you can have your own room here, you can come and work here."[27]

And so he did.

Above left: Soutine and Madeleine; Above right: Soutine's 1925 *Enfant de choeur* was one of Madeleine and Marcellin's first paintings by the artist, and Madeleine's favorite; Opposite: Soutine captured his patroness here in about 1929. It took six sittings for the portrait's completion. Madeleine described being painted by Soutine as a savage experience.

LÈVES

"Lèves, it was a whole life."

MICHEL CASTAING

The mysterious house behind the stone wall had captured the young Madeleine's imagination as a school girl and continued to haunt her. Years later, in 1924, she finally made it hers. Madeleine recalled her reunion with the beloved house which only war and death could wrest from her:

> Just after we got married, I talked to my husband about it and we decided to go back to those places from my childhood. We climbed over the wall. I was tremendously disappointed: the property was a wasteland taken over by brambles. But there was an abandoned house with a tree growing through the roof. I decided that I would own that house; I wanted it with all my might.[1]

Marcellin's first reaction after surveying its derelict condition was, "Tu rêves," ("In your dreams") but, as usual, it didn't take her long to secure his approval. As with all of her passions, such as Soutine's *Garçon de choeur* and even Marcellin, it was an instantaneous and enduring love.

If Lèves offered a retreat from the incessant social whirl of Paris, it has also been suggested that it was a way to keep Marcellin under Madeleine's watchful eye and away from the long-legged temptations of the city. From 1928 to 1933, the Castaings lived at Lèves exclusively. Marcellin, now retired with the rents from his family's various properties able to sustain their comfortable lifestyle, played tennis and read prodigiously while Madeleine threw herself into transforming Lèves into the vision of her dreams. The writer Maurice Sachs, who was a friend and frequent visitor, paid tribute to Madeleine and her creation: "Attractive, perceptive, biased, happy, put-together, disorderly, obstinate, she had a kind of creative genius for everything related to houses. With a charming Directoire lantern lighting the old walls of the chateau of the Bishop of Chartres, she made a home full of fantasy, innovation, and boldness; and on the uncultivated land that surrounded it, she designed a beautiful park that seemed like it had always been there."[2]

Just like her grandparents' house the Villa des Roses in Saint-Prest, the doors of Lèves welcomed a steady stream of the Castaings' friends. Concerts, readings, and promenades on the grounds were all part of a weekend's entertainment.

During the 1930s, Soutine spent months at a time at Lèves. "We had an intense desire: to see

The former country house of the bishops of Chartres captivated Madeleine the moment she first laid eyes on it as a young school girl. She transformed every inch of the property over several decades, and it was without doubt her masterpiece.

him paint. And we lived for that and that alone. We thought about it when we woke up, we thought about it at night while we were falling asleep: seeing him paint."[3] On the rare occasion that a completed work met with Soutine's approval, then and only then would he invite the Castaings to view it. Madeleine remembered, "It was what Marcellin called the 'viewing ceremony.' It was extremely nerve-racking because we knew that if the look on our faces wasn't laudatory enough, the bottle of turpentine was right there and he'd wipe everything away. But when the painting was a success, it was pure bliss."[4] Madeleine always held this time of her life as a profoundly special one.

Much like the empress Josephine's country house Malmaison, the Neoclassical Lèves is imbued with the formal elegance of the Directoire period, but its modest size conveyed an intimate coziness. Built in 1793 on the ruins of a medieval *maison forte*, the house is painted the color of the sky,[5] hung with turquoise shutters, and surmounted by a triangular temple pediment centered by a lunette of a seated classical maiden. Swags and recessed busts supported on corbel brackets are the only relief to the restrained facade. A double staircase engulfed in ivy ascends to the piano nobile which is centered by a balustraded elliptical bay opening to the *salon de la rotonde*.

The romantic atmosphere of Lèves is due in no small part to its picturesque setting. Madeleine concentrated as much energy on carefully shaping the fifteen acres of grounds as she did on the house itself. Her desire to connect the indoors to the outside is vital to understanding Castaing style. This is why she often paired the blue of the sky with the greens of grass and foliage—an unpopular color combination at the time, but yet one found in nature. (However one element of the outdoors Madeleine had no interest in having in her rooms was floods of sunlight. She went to great lengths to control the interior light levels at Lèves, even going so far as to tent both levels of the terrace by suspending muslin from above the uppermost window so that the she could diffuse the light on both floors![6])

Allées of poplars lined up with the windows and extended the boundaries of rooms; luxuriant willows reminiscent of Scarlet O'Hara's Tara moodily draped themselves over the river that ran through the property and created fairy tale settings in which to daydream. Underneath the terrace was what Madeleine called the Nymphaeum, after the female stone busts arranged on pedestals between the arcaded piers. Here family and guests gathered in the shade for leisurely amusements. Her son Michel recalled her constantly walking the grounds with her clippers, trimming and train-ing ivy so it produced the desired effect[7]: to look as if it had always been there.

Madeleine painted Lèves's facade pale blue and the shutters a brilliant turquoise. The bay windows of the *salon de la rotonde* opened directly onto a terrace. Ivy picturequely cascaded down the terrace and stairs.

Madeleine was always roaming the grounds of Lèves with her clippers in hand. She planned all the allées to line up with the house's windows and provide a verdant foliate-framed view.

An abandoned rusted wheelbarrow beautifully illustrates the poetic vignettes that Madeleine was so talented at fashioning; Following: The Nymphaeum, so-called because of the busts of classical maidens parading around the piers, was a place where guests gathered for impromptu entertainments.

Maurice Sachs was mesmerized by Madeleine's efforts:

The constant transformations she made to the estate kept her as busy as the world can keep a socialite. She spent so much time with the plants and the gardeners that she had to steal away to get to the antique stores. She'd come back running, as late as an adulterous woman, but her sprees were for a sideboard, an armchair, a display cabinet. They'd eat at any time of the day; they'd get up to run go see a painting. That woman amazed me because she worked on her happiness like an artist works on his masterpiece.[8]

"Although Julietta's room was a room in which time stopped . . . . The candlelight and the deep shadows, the flowers and their scent, the heaping plates of fruit, round cakes, and compotes, everything seemed like it was from an imaginary land."[9]

Just as she famously ordered clothes to *her* design at the *maisons de couture* of Dior and Balenciaga, Madeleine displayed from the beginning her disinterest in the prevailing trends of the day. The abstracted Neoclassicism of Art Deco and the minimalism of the International Style held no fascination for her. Instead, she created her own distinctive look out of a mélange of styles, woven together with wit and fantasy. Lèves is without question Madeleine's masterpiece and the supreme example of *le style* Castaing.

Vines of ivy, often fake—or "make-believe," as she preferred to call it—encircling a chandelier or compote; a hand of playing cards laid out; books propped open randomly—these were all theatrical effects that breathed life into a room, hinting that someone had just left or would shortly be returning. It has been said that Madeleine's style was the style of her childhood, of the Third Republic, when progress was cloaked in densely furnished and upholstered rooms in which comfort reigned supreme. Over-upholstered and tufted seat furniture applied with rows of fringe and trim found their way into almost every Castaing space. Another nineteenth-century quotation was the patterned carpets of ivy, banana leaves, or flowers—which, when used by her decades later, take on a surreal quality. To instill a house with one's essence—or to make it a mirror, as she put it—is to connect it to memory. By evoking the past, an experiential dimension is added to the room. As Marcel Proust captured in his famous passage on a madeleine, an everyday object, scent, or taste can transport one back, in both memory and feeling, to another time and place.

Her personal attachment to the nineteenth century stemmed from her grandparents' Villa des Roses, where so many powerful childhood memories were formed, as well as from the novels of Balzac, Stendhal, and Zola whose detailed descriptions of interiors and material culture ignited Madeleine's visual imagination. In these novels, the decoration and furnishings of a room are a manifestation of the character of its inhabitant so that, as in the case of Madame de Mortsauf, the heroine of Balzac's *Le Lys dans la vallée,* her supremely simple but elegant salon is as "calm and collected as the life of the countess":

> . . . then I took her hand again and looked long at the brown and gray room, the simple bed with curtains of chintz, the table covered with a toilet-cloth trimmed in the old-fashioned way, the shabby sofa with quilted cushion. What poetry in this spot! What neglect of luxury for herself! Her luxury was the most exquisite cleanliness. Noble cell of a religious wife full of saintly resignation, in which the only ornament was the bedside crucifix, above which was the portrait of her aunt; then, on each side of the holy water font, pencil drawings of her two children done by herself, and their hair from the time they were little. What a retreat for a woman whose appearance in the fashionable world would have thrown the fairest into the shade! Such was the boudoir where the daughter of an illustrious house ever mourned, just now overwhelmed with bitterness and denying herself the love which would have consoled her.[10]

Lèves may have been her remembrance of time passed, but Madeleine's way of combining unlikely elements was so fresh—and perhaps purposely perverse—that it immediately caused a stir. Unfortunately, photos of the house with its first scheme before the Germans requisitioned it in 1940 have not been found. By 1943, Lèves had been sold[11] and it isn't until the 1950s, well after Madeleine had already established herself as an antiques dealer and decorator, that we get our first glimpse inside the house of her dreams.

Madeleine recalled years later how brutally their bucolic life was interrupted by World War II: "I remember. I had just changed the curtains and had put flowers all around the house. We were living in our own world; we wouldn't even open the letters we got in the mail. I hardly knew that there was a war going on. All of a sudden soldiers in blue-green got through to the garden and wrecked the beds. My whole poetic universe had suddenly collapsed."[12]

The war also brought an end to the Castaings' golden years dedicated to supporting the genius of Soutine. As a well-known Jewish artist, Soutine went into hiding during the Nazi occupation of France. When his chronic stomach problems became severe, he underwent an unsuccessful operation. Soon after, in August 1943, he died of a perforated ulcer. According to Madeleine, the Castaings followed the painter's work until his last days and were profoundly saddened by his death.

Four years after the conclusion of the war in 1949, Madeleine finally had the opportunity to reclaim Lèves. By this time, the house was in the hands of a local farmers' union who agreed to trade it in exchange for another piece of property. Marcellin refused to contribute a centime, so with the gains from her thriving shop, Madeleine bought Lèves back with her own money. It was now truly *hers*. "So she acquired a property in Normandy, Les Minimes [to trade], and she could finally settle down again in her enchanted realm. Her joy was indescribable. In a blink of an eye, there was a boat on the river in Lèves for a long time on which she had painted the inscription 'Les Minimes,'" recounted her daughter-in-law Josette.[13]

After recovering and restoring the house with the help of the architect Raymond Robain and

a local mason, she decided to completely redecorate and refurnish it with the intent that every room recall and harmonize with the landscape. Here she experimented with colors, patterns, and styles—it was the genesis of *le style* Castaing. She compared the process to poetry and indeed, she didn't then nor ever approach her schemes with a predetermined battle plan, much less a furniture plan. Every weekend a truck came out with her week's finds at the flea markets and an orchestration of movers placed and replaced the pieces until a poetic arrangement was made.

It was in the mid-1930s that Madeleine earned the nickname "reine des Puces." She explained:

> Every morning at 8:00, and God knows I'm not a morning person, I rode my bike rain or shine to the Marché Jules-Vallès. It was the most squalid part of the flea market, a real wasteland. The ground was covered with clinker so you didn't step in the mud and you'd come back at night black with coal dust kicked up by the wind. In shacks made out of dilapidated planks, old central European immigrants resold all the knick-knacks that they had bought in the auction room. People fought; they grabbed things out of each other's hands. I would come back loaded with purchases that I'd tuck away in storage.[14]

An item wasn't purchased with an idea for a specific spot or because it was of outstanding quality; rather, she bought what charmed and intrigued her only to be determined later where it should go. The items that didn't work—Madeleine joked that she bought enough to furnish Lèves ten times over—were stored in a space on the rue du Cherche-Midi. "I don't care if a piece of furniture is 'good.' What interests me is its secret life, which only becomes apparent in an ideal ensemble, in a kind of perfect harmony."[15] Her love of romance did make her susceptible to provenance, and she would take great pleasure in a pair of chaises longues that had belonged to Pauline Borghese or a stool on ballerina legs which she claimed originated from a bordello.

As important as the element of fantasy to Madeleine's roomscapes were comfort and practicality, and one article notes that every detail was thought of by Lèves's chatelaine: the patterned leopard carpet that hid muddy footsteps; a well-stocked bar tucked behind a blind arch in the corner of the salon; the guest rooms outfitted with assorted furniture and trays to unpack one's wardrobe with ease.

What is astonishing about comparing photographs of the house taken over a span of four decades is how little it changed. Signs of tweaking and refining are apparent; for example, new fabric for curtains in the dining room, or a different mirror placed over the mantel in the salon—but it is clear, that once Madeleine was satisfied with a room, she remained so. This constancy—of vision, purpose, and attachment—perhaps explains the determination and great success of a person who was also a dreamer and fantasist.

The centerpiece of the first floor was the magnificent *salon de la rotonde*, which combined three spaces into one grand one. To create cohesiveness between the three delineated areas, she

Preceding: Madeleine used dark grey paint to draw out the Neoclassical architectural elements in the *salon de la rotonde*. The chimneypiece was flanked by two arches—one leading into the Winter Bedroom, the other fitted with shelves for a bar; Opposite: Madeleine strategically used the graphic leopard-patterned carpet for the entire salon: It unified the three spaces of the room and masked any dirty footprints tracked in from the grounds.

used a leopard carpet from Maison Hamot. Interestingly, by 1953, the walls of the round bay in the center of the salon which opened to the terrace were dramatically upholstered in deep crimson velvet en suite with banquettes that hugged the curving wall. This striking color choice was perhaps meant to complement and heighten the greens of the foliage seen beyond. Later she changed the wall hangings to her signature blue bordered by a palmette frieze of green, black, and white taken from a Directoire document fabric. Two seating areas, one in front of the chimneypiece and the other set around bookcases, flanked the rounded center with a bay of large French doors opening onto the terrace. Madeleine created a structured, balanced furniture arrangement which both unified and articulated each area and, key to appreciating her style and talent, in a way that looked organic and effortless. To anchor the arrangement, a circular settee was placed in the center on axis with the doors leading outside.

Beyond the library was the dining room which beautifully exemplified Madeleine's blurring of the in- and out-of-doors. The opaline blue walls had several floor-to-ceiling windows which looked out onto lush verdant greenery. On a pier, *Une allée au printemps*, an oil by Soutine, acted as a virtual window, introducing more green foliage into the space. At the other end of the first floor was the White or Winter Bedroom.

The walls of the bedroom were hung with cotton printed with floral-sprigged foliage cascading down in stripes. Its design was inspired by the allées that Madeleine had planted on the grounds of Lèves. She imagined the fabric, now known as "Rayure Fleurie," continuing the view from the window so that there was no interruption from window to wall. A white tented ceiling embellished with bobble trim and a bed canopied in white muslin cocooned and cosseted the space. As always, the emphasis on feminine comfort was balanced by the severe lines of the Neoclassical furniture. An earlier scheme of the bedroom deployed a favorite Indian floral chintz, used several times elsewhere by Madeleine for clients,[16] for the walls and bedcovering. A densely floral-patterned carpet preceded the later sprigged diamond one.

A long hallway spanned the entire width of the house from which one can enter any of the rooms on the first floor or ascend to the second floor. The walls were painted an ochre faux marble, arranged in panels, and the floors of white and black stone laid on the diagonal. A banquette and assorted lightweight chairs furnish the passage as if it were a room of its own, not just a vestibule to pass through. The staircase is covered in a wool carpet of deep greens, greys, and blues in banana leaves of Madeleine's own design.

Upstairs were four bedrooms and an informal salon. Madeleine's, the largest with a spacious sitting room attached, is located directly over the central rotunda. Dubbed the Pink, or Summer, Bedroom it appears bathed in a pink glow, like the inside of a shell, created by bright pink painted

Preceding: Picturesque views were framed by gauzy white muslin in the bay of the *salon de la rotonde;* Opposite: A photograph from the early 1950s captured an earlier decorating scheme of the salon. The Napoleon III "borne" holding court in the middle of the room also got a makeover later on. Here it is covered in blue "Rayure Broderie."

Preceding: Two arched niches painted to recall the sky enclose petite console tables supporting large blue urns overflowing with "make-believe" flowers in the center of the salon; Madeleine "expanded" a Regency mahogany bookcase to create the library corner in the salon.

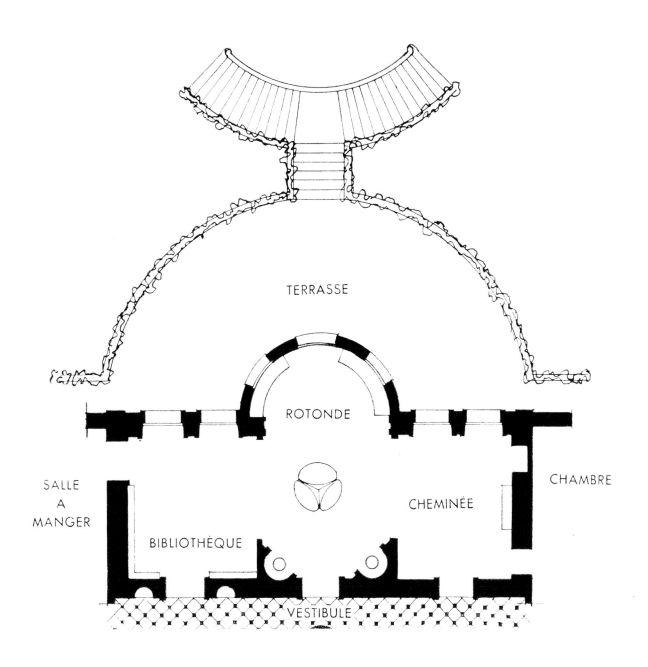

TERRASSE

ROTONDE

SALLE
A
MANGER

CHAMBRE

CHEMINÉE

BIBLIOTHÈQUE

VESTIBULE

A floor plan of the first floor of Lèves; Following: In the dining room, Soutine's *L'arbe de Vence* acts as an additional window to the outdoors.
The deep brown mahogany of the English Regency furniture, the sky blue walls, and foliate patterned carpeting evokes a picnic *en plein air*.

The Winter Bedroom off of the salon was hung with "Rayure Fleurie," a floral-garland-striped fabric of Madeleine's creation that continued the views of the garden's allées onto the walls.

The tenting of the ceiling and the swan-headed iron bed were an unmistakable bow to the elegant style of Napoleon's consort Josephine.

Above and opposite: The vestibule spanned the entire facade of the house and, in classic Castaing fashion, was furnished with banquettes and chairs as if it was a room to linger in, not just pass through. Classically proportioned grey and ochre trompe l'oeil marbleized panels articulated the walls.

Following: The master bedroom on the second floor opened out onto a small balustraded terrace where Madeleine and Marcellin breakfasted in the summer. Deep pink painted walls glowed through the shirred muslin.

A large black-painted Biedermeier *secretaire a abattant* adds a splash of drama and provides a strong counterpoint to the frothy pinks and creams used throughout the bedroom.

In Madeleine's bathroom, an unusual small chair is supported on ballerina legs *en pointe*. It was reputedly from a brothel and its quirky charm and provenance would have been irresistible to Madeleine; Following: Floral chintz festooned the sitting area of the Summer or Pink Bedroom.

Arrangements of silhouettes were artfully hung throughout this guest bedroom. The deep leafy green of the floral print was repeated in the picked out paneling of the cupboard doors.

A small corbel bracket ingeniously served as a lamp stand between the two twin beds; Following: In this library-cum-lounge on the second floor, bottle green velvet curtains and "Eglantine" carpet suggest a woodland retreat.

walls overlaid with white muslin, just like the boudoir of *La fille aux yeux d'or*[17], by Balzac, who described the overall effect:

> Never was richness more coquettishly veiled to become elegance, to express grace, to inspire voluptuousness. Here everything would have warmed the heart of even the coldest being. The way the hangings shimmered, their color always changing according to your gaze, becoming either completely white, or completely pink, harmonized with the effects of the light infused in the diaphanous folds of chiffon, producing a misty appearance.[18]

The adjacent sitting room, hung with a large scale Restoration-style floral chintz of pinks and dark greens on a creamy white ground, is where Madeleine and Marcellin breakfasted during the summer. Madeleine's love of black painted furniture added a strong counterpoint to the confectionary prettiness and plush upholstered surroundings.

The small guest bedroom repeated the "blue-and-green" sky and grass theme. Muslin-hung walls were paired with a blue and green floral cotton trimmed in green used for the twin bedcoverings and curtains. The same glazed cotton was used on the ceilings and walls of the adjoining bathroom and like Nancy Lancaster in England, Madeleine is credited with launching the vogue in France for fully furnishing bathrooms as any other room.[19]

One striking commonality shared by all of Madeleine's rooms is that one doesn't know where or when one is. Is it 1840s Russia, or 1950s France, or even 2004, when the contents of Madeleine's residences and store were auctioned by Sotheby's? It is interesting to note that the origins of many of the over 700 lots in the sale were difficult to catalogue. Instead of a full attribution, they are merely recorded as "nineteenth century," and it is this elusiveness that contributed greatly to the Castaing interior. Its out-of-time, out-of-place quality.

Although Lèves was her greatest creation, Madeleine saw her marriage of over five decades to Marcellin as her most important achievement. "Looking after, building love is like building a cathedral. Oh, what you have to expend—a treasure trove of inventions, mischief, tenderness, restraint, sacrifice—to captivate a man! Fifty-two years of passion …. Nothing else I did matters."[20] After Marcellin's death in 1966, Madeleine no longer liked to stay overnight at Lèves. Instead she would drive down from Paris for the day. Upon arriving, if the light or the mood or some other ineffable quality wasn't just right, Madeleine would decide that it wasn't meant to be, and immediately order the car back to town.

Marcellin, here in his fifties, with Bernard, left, and Michel, right, who wear the white gloves and white armbands of their First Communion.

ACT TWO: MADELEINE THE MERCHANT

"Julietta. First chapter. To invent well it's wise to not know anything."[1] LOUISE DE VILMORIN, *Julietta* (1953)

"I was early, that's all. I've always done what I like and I've always had the courage of my convictions," Madeleine said once. It takes a certain entrepreneurial spirit and moxy to see opportunity in the face of adversity; stripped of almost everything she loved best, Madeleine showed she had it in spades. With her beloved Lèves commandeered by the Germans and later sold, Madeleine and Marcellin were now in Paris full-time where there was no escaping the devastating turn of world events. In the darkest days of wartime, Madeleine tapped into the creative energy she had concentrated on the decoration of Lèves and channeled it into a new venture through which she could distill and disseminate *le style* Castaing—all the while making a profit.

Although it was never directly addressed by Madeleine, there appears to have been a need for additional income. Perhaps the rents which supported the Castaings were frozen during the occupation or the assets themselves seized, but Madeleine hints that it was necessity—and not mere whim—that prompted her to go into trade. "It was in 1940: the debacle, the Germans 30 kilometers outside of Chartres, and a telephone call in the middle of the night. Marcellin picks up the phone and he says, 'I'll accept it.' I say to him, 'You'll accept what?' 'Someone made an offer for *Le Pâtissier* [a painting by Soutine lent to an exhibition in New York].' And Marcellin had said yes, he was selling it." Furious, Madeleine vowed this would be the first and last Soutine sold: "What if they all go? I'm going to work!"[3]

Madeleine's grandson Frédéric Castaing describes how the ravaging of Lèves further propelled her towards this decision: "Lèves had been occupied by the Germans, who destroyed everything .... Actually they didn't destroy everything, but I mean they beat up the place .... On top of that, after the Liberation, the house had been ransacked, so it was in ruins. And my grandfather was so sick about it that in short, he wanted to sell it."[4]

Madeleine recalled of those years in Paris:

> Paris was sad and empty. The interiors were sad, very sad. And I needed above all to say how I saw the houses and how I liked them to be. And Maurice was there, Maurice Sachs, a friend, who would say to me, "Madeleine, express yourself. Madeleine, we need you. Madeleine, breathe some life into all these houses. Let yourself go."

Madeleine recumbent in stripes and wearing one of the fanciful hats that was her signature until she adopted the famous wig strap. It wasn't until her late forties that Madeleine began her career as antiquaire and decorator.

To open a business at the height of wartime in her late forties without ever having worked a day in her life was audacious to say the least. But as always when Madeleine made up her mind, her unwavering confidence brooked no obstacles. Her first foray into selling her amassment of wares was a stand at the marché Jules-Vallès located in the huge Clignancourt complex in the northern outskirts of Paris. Together with Jacques Damiot, a young man who had grown up in Chartres and had accompanied her on her buying adventures for Lèves, their stand soon attracted attention and success. By the beginning of 1941, she was ready to take it to the next level.[5]

A space on the rue du Cherche-Midi previously rented to store the furnishings purchased on her incessant buying sprees spurred an idea:

> After one of those shopping sprees that I'm known for, I had rented, without knowing what I'd do with it, a shop on rue du Cherche-Midi that had belonged to Madame Sans-Gêne [Mrs. Ill-mannered].[6] We decided to set it up. I hung the curtains myself, put the bookcase up, and with the harmonious, practical English furniture that I've always liked, I recreated a novelistic home. Intrigued by seeing this shop transformed into a Balzacien room, passers-by piled up in front of the window. Some of them came in to find out more.

Ingeniously Madeleine, who had no interest in being a shopkeeper, treated the various rooms of the boutique as if it were a residence.

> For two weeks I worked on the library, two weeks later I made a bedroom, two weeks later I did something else, but I made a real home. I noticed that the first few times that someone came into my shop, I rushed up the stairs—my heart was pounding and pounding. There was nothing you could do to get me to come back down. I wouldn't do it. And then I started to get used to it. And I would go down and I'd have conversations with the people who came in, we got along well, they were delighted, they would come back the next day. And it was an immediate success.[7]

Those walking by couldn't help but to stop and stare in the windows. The blurring between a commercial space and a private residence was deliberate and extremely clever in two respects: not only did it grab the attention of would-be voyeurs passing by, but it showcased how an item might look at home, complete with tea services set out and opened books cast here and there. She is credited with being the first to display wares in this way, and even though the label may have made her bristle, she was a merchandising pioneer.

Madeleine's eye for the eclectic distinguished her establishment immediately. "These princesses put some of their historic, signed furniture away in the attic and replaced them with a wicker armchair or a *bibelot* they saw at my place. The French needed to escape the grim reality of the occupation. I provided that escape for them."[8] An early admirer, Christian "Bébé" Bérard, brought many from his fashionable set through and word soon spread about the charming installations chez Madame Castaing. Her friend Domenica Walter, the widow of prolific art dealer Paul

Madeleine shows off her mastery at mixing patterns: her "Branches de Pin" print on the walls and soft furnishings was boldly paired with "Léopard" on the floor in her rue Bonaparte shop in the 1950s.

Guillaume, also gave great encouragement to Madeleine in the beginning and brought some of her first clients to the Cherche-Midi premises.

Flush with success, Madeleine moved her premises to 21, rue Bonaparte in April 1946. From the beginning, she made a splash: She had the facade painted black, causing her neighbors to cattily comment that a funeral parlor had opened. Its layout as a series of succeeding small rooms was ideal for Madeleine's mise en scènes, but most likely what charmed Madeleine most were its architectural bones of Neoclassical niches and colonettes reminiscent of Lèves. Over time, Madeleine bought adjacent shops and expanded her premises along the intersecting rue Jacob. Even her storerooms located throughout the neighborhood didn't escape her decorating fantasies and might be arrayed as a winter garden or some other whimsical arrangement.

Just as on the rue du Cherche-Midi, she treated the shop as if it were a living doll house; each space was fully dressed as a room with much thought lavished on the props to make it come to life, whether it entailed decanters of whisky in the library or pens and paper on a desk. "I was the first one to do that. There are a lot of people who do the same thing now, but they don't make it seem like there's life there, like there's someone living there …."[9]

Opposite: Every detail was thought of in this dining room vignette in Madeleine's shop, c. 1957, including two of her own Soutines. Red velvet walls and her "Castaing Cachemire" carpet in green and black provide further zing to the mise-en-scène; Above: The proud proprietor stands outside her shop at the intersection of the rues Jacob and Bonaparte. She and Marcellin lived on the mezzanine level directly overhead.

Preceding: A view of Madeleine's shop taken after her death when it was under the direction of her longtime assistant, Laure Lombardini; Above: Swatches of Madeleine's own fabric line, which contributed significantly to her business' bottom line, are at the ready.

An Imari porcelain teacup sat on a tufted and swagged banquette as if waiting for its mistress to return.

"The room was full of Nana's intimate life: a pair of her gloves, a fallen handkerchief, an open book lay scattered about, evoking an impression of their owner en déshabillé, in the midst of her scent of violets and that happy-go-lucky untidiness which created such a charming effect in these rich surroundings." [10]

Breathing life into a room was Madeleine's particular genius, and ironically, it was looking to literature of the nineteenth century which inspired her outside-of-time and timeless mise en scènes.

> I sat down there. The shop had just closed. I was alone, the best part of the day. The last hints of soft autumn sunlight gave the room a bluish tint. I thought of the Chartreuse de Parme, the Duchesse Sanseverina. I imagined her in blue quilted décor, sinking into this soft couch, drinking her coffee at this mahogany table. I worked until the middle of the night. Bit by bit the idea of an atmosphere and of the furniture came together. [11]
>
> The billiard room could be Monsieur de Custine's library, the button-padded corner makes you think of Princess Mathilde, the pipes are Alexandre Dumas', the other armchair is Balzacien, and the pair of bookshelves could very well have belonged to Byron. [12]

If Balzac's detailed descriptions of rooms evoked images in her mind's eye, nineteenth-century watercolors of interiors brought them to life. From a young age, Madeleine had observed closely the art of furnishing and decorating[13] and she paid the same close attention to these portraits of a period. However, she had no interest in creating a period room: "I always tell my clients that above all we should not try to create an interior from another time period."[14]

Without a further thought to purity of style or period, Madeleine introduced Biedermeier, Russian, and English Regency cheek-by-jowl with Napoleon III and the random piece made of antlers or bone. "Mixing allows you to avoid reconstruction. It injects life into a grouping."[15] Just as she introduced a new appreciation for the English Regency style, she was an early proponent of Russian furniture. In the 1960s, Madeleine began buying wares from the White Russian aristocrats whose destitution forced them to sell their fine furniture. Even though she never traveled there, Russia had a great enchantment for Madeleine. The home of countless writers and painters as well as a glittery

Madeleine knew that it was the small details, both humble and gilt, that made a room come to life.

court that was dramatically and tragically deposed undoubtedly appealed to her romantic nature.

Her eclecticism of period, style, and quality was in stark contrast to the prevailing ethos of connoisseurship and provenance emphasized by other dealers. She regarded nothing as sacred—she would lacquer something black or change a wooden table top to one of marble without hesitation. What mattered was the overall effect.

Indeed so little did Madeleine care about such things that one of her clients joked that if a chair had a broken leg, it must have come from Madeleine's shop.[16] Her disregard of condition was known to put her at loggerheads with her upholsterer Roland Seigneur. He remembers: "What she didn't like either was when you'd tell her that a chair was busted, that the trim was too old, that it was too old. Oh, for her, it was always very good. 'You just have to recover it with new fabric, right?' And my father, he was a little upset with her because he refused to re-cover just anything. It wasn't always easy."[17]

Flying in the face of conventional notions of good taste is something Madeleine perhaps deliberately pursued. Her embrace of the deeply unfashionable Napoleon III style has struck some as having an air of rebellion to it. Similarly, her desire to place something bizarre or ugly in a room may also be attributed to her desire to do the unexpected. Whether or not there was an intentional motivation to provoke, what is beyond question was her love of imperfection, or conversely her horror of perfection. After a room was freshly painted, she was known to have put a vacuum cleaner on reverse to add instant patina to the walls and to take a curtain off a rung or two so that there was instantaneously a lived-in look. She explained this entirely singular approach:

> What I've brought to it is ease in letting go: colors that were once forbidden and that are now accepted, the unexpected, the opposite of convention. And yes, part of it is always chance. I introduced mystery; there was never mystery in houses. You can feel mystery; it comes from a certain beauty. There's always beauty in mystery. The unexpected is always there and it brings things to life.[18]

MERCHANDISING THE CASTAING LOOK

"My braids, fabrics, and carpets are the colours of my palette, but I can take inspiration from a scene in Chekov as from a dress by Goya."[19]

Every object in Madeleine's shop had to capture her eye and imagination for it to find a place in one of her schemes.

Pivotal to creating and branding the Castaing look were her own trademark designs for fabric, carpeting, and furniture. Diversifying her business with subsidiary lines was another instance of her acumen as well as one of the most lucrative sources of income. That she didn't have a formal education in design was no obstacle—she preferred motifs and patterns that had history behind them anyway. She collected vintage and antique textiles and tweaked them, often reimagining them in fresh, clear colors. For her line of fabrics and carpets, she collaborated with the storied firm of Maison Hamot who had their own extensive archives stretching back to their founding in 1762 from which she could cull as well.

In the instances when an "original" concept struck—which was every other minute as she was a font of inspiration—she would describe her ideas to her friend François Hamot who then translated them into cloth. Apparently never without a pair of scissors, she was always ready to clip a swatch of whatever captivated her attention, such as the blue of a Venetian vaporetto's curtain, and bring it back to Hamot to copy. A brilliant red Russian cashmere shawl spied in a shop window so struck Madeleine that she waited hours for the proprietor's return until she made it hers. The rich red and woven borders of the shawl found their way onto "Rayure Cachemire." Another signature pattern "Rayure Fleurie," born out of Madeleine's philosophy of connecting the indoors and outside, was meant to continue the allées of trees seen out the window onto the wall.

In a mutually beneficial arrangement, one could only buy the Castaing lines in France and the rest of Europe directly from Madeleine herself, whereas Hamot had the rights to distribute elsewhere, including the United States where she had a tremendous following. The names by which her most celebrated fabrics are known were not bestowed by her. "Rayure Cachemire" was fittingly "Le Chale" ("the shawl"); the Empire style "Dentelle" was "Faille moiré dentelle"; and "Rayure Broderie" she called "Rayure Balzac."[20] Most of her designs were printed on cotton, with only "Dentelle" available in moiré.

An undeniable love of and sensitivity to pattern is apparent in her carpeting choices. She didn't blink at mixing patterned walls with a differently patterned floor. She didn't care for "eastern" carpets[21] and indeed wall-to-wall or a fifty centimeter perimeter from the wall was generally the rule in her schemes. The floors of her first shop were covered with nineteenth-century ivy-patterned carpet from the French Senate which she purchased at auction for a song. This may have been the initial inspiration behind her floral and fauna carpeting designs, such as one of her most frequently used, Eglantine.

When Madeleine struck on something that pleased her, she stayed faithful and so it was with the collection of her fabrics and carpets which she reused over and over again for decades. She adhered to the same colorways, but did allow Hamot to occasionally offer variations, such as a

A few of Madeleine's signature fabrics: from top left, clockwise, "Rayure Cachemire," "Dentelle," "Rayure Broderie," and "Rayure Fleurie." Her favorite colors blue, green, and red with touches of black dominated her designs.

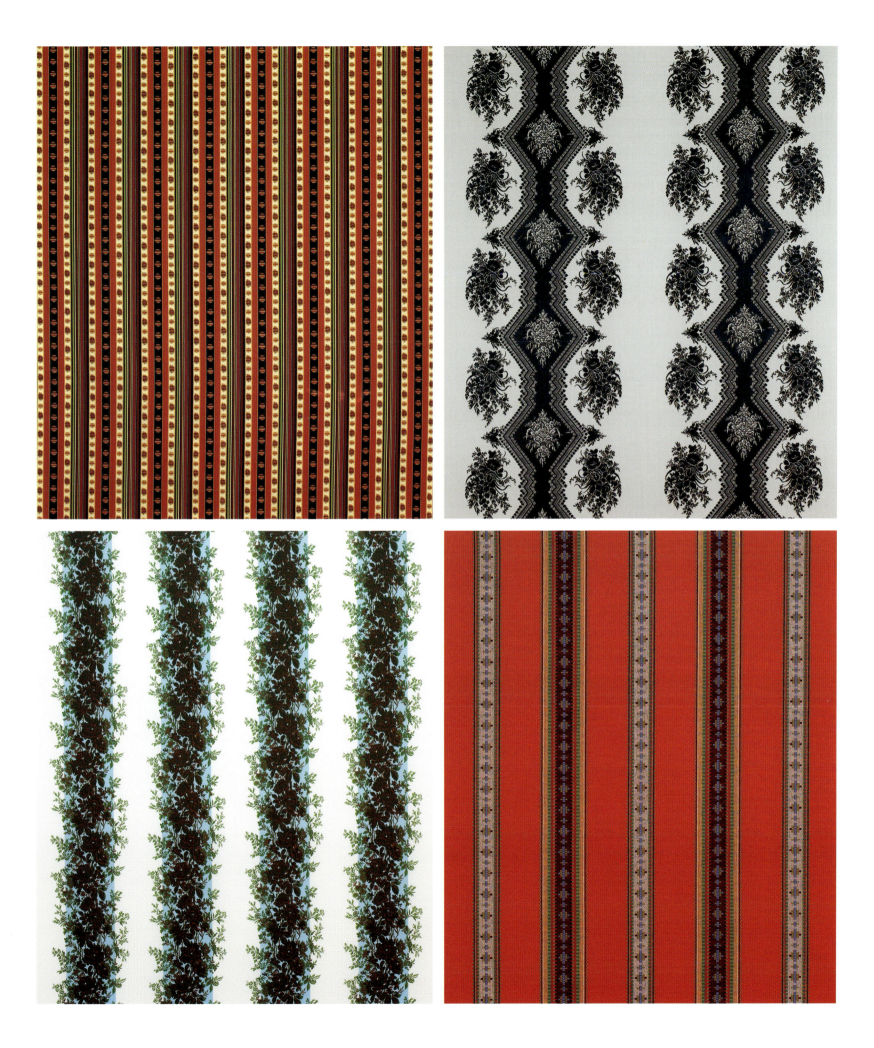

The "Léopard" patterned carpet Madeleine used to singular effect at Lèves and elsewhere may have seemed a bold choice, but it was one that had historical antecedents in Josephine's own schemes.

In the empress' dining room at the Château de Compiègne, decorated under the direction of Josephine herself in the opening decade of the nineteenth century, leopard carpeting was employed.

version of Coppelia which incorporated an additional blue. It should be noted that not all of the stuffs she used were from her own line. The leopard carpeting with which she has become so identified and a favorite Indian chintz used several times were part of Hamot's existing inventory.

"I use three colors: red, sky blue, and the green of the gardens; but all colors are beautiful if they're in harmony."[22] But it is for that haunting hue which lies between a turquoise and verdigris that is famously called "bleu Castaing." Its invention may have been by chance: Bouchardeau, the firm that manufactured her lampshades, credit one of their papers as being the origins of the famous shade.[23]

There is a daring behind her choices—to put blue with green was completely unconventional and a little jarring, but as the colors of "le ciel et la verdure" they of course went together. However, it might be more accurate to say she employed four colors: red, blue, green, and black. Black-painted furniture or bordered motifs on her fabrics and carpets added punch and weight to her rooms. Its force acted as a masculine counterpoint to the feminine tufting and passementerie of her schemes.

By adhering strictly to a limited color palette and range of textiles and carpets, she created an immediately identifiable look. Her colleagues in the trade criticized her continuity: "She never stops repeating the same couches that Count Mosca goes to sit on, the same old maid padded rooms."[24]

Also available for purchase chez Castaing were her signature lampshades. Always of the same conical shape, small in proportion and lined in gold foil for a warm cast, they were mounted on all manner of gas lamps and candlesticks. (The notion of converting a vase or object into a lamp whose original function wasn't for illumination was considered a *faute de goût*.) Lighting was extremely important to her. She took great care to study samples at different times, noting how it changed during the course of a day. Electric light, which she could control and orchestrate into poetic pools, was preferred to daylight. Sheers or the nineteenth-century roller shades handpainted with birds, flowers, and foliage were often employed to filter natural light.

THE GAME OF SELLING

None of the items in her shop had price tags, and if the uninitiated asked to purchase an item, most likely he was given one of two answers: an astronomical price or that the item was beyond price and couldn't possibly be sold. It is true that Madeleine's carefully composed vignettes would suffer if one of their components was taken away; it is also true—to a degree—that she opened a shop not because she wanted to sell, but because she liked to buy and make poetic settings out of her acquisitions.

However, one can't discount Madeleine's innate canniness and her understanding of how much

Bright light could kill the mood of enchantment Madeleine worked carefully to conjure. Nineteenth-century roller blinds, hand-painted with fanciful flora and fauna, were often called to arms to filter daylight.

more desirable something becomes when it is out of reach. In any case, she knew that an item is worth as much as one values it, and everything Madeleine bought and displayed she enthusiastically regarded. Stories abound of clients returning several times to plead their case over a certain chair or vase, until she finally relented—at a price, of course! In this excerpt from a conversation with François-Marie Banier, Madeleine recounts one of her classically quixotic interactions with clients:

> MADELEINE CASTAING: One of my good clients who just bought a tremendous amount of things last month: "I beg you, I'd like to give it [a Barbotine] to my wife for Christmas." So I said there was no way, that it's the most beautiful Barbotine that I've ever seen in my life and that I was keeping it. So of course, it's going to be a bidding war. But I say maybe.

> FRANÇOIS-MARIE BANIER: How much is it worth? Three thousand francs? It's worth three thousand francs.

> MC: No, I'd let it go for five million, not a cent less.

> FMB: And you said three million just now.

> MC: Just now, but I change quickly.

> FMB: And always a higher price?

> MC: Or I don't change at all.

> FMB: What do you mean, not at all?

> MC: Not at all. I say, "No. No, I'm unfortunately obligated to keep it. Obligated to keep it. I'm very sorry. But maybe I'll change my mind. Come back in 6 months or a year."

> FMB: And people aren't furious?

> MC: No, they come back. They come back. And they say, "Thank you." And they always come back.

> FMB: They can't pay five million for an object that's worth three thousand francs.

> MC: But . . . here's the thing. Three thousand francs. Why three thousand francs? Why three million? Why? Ask the object.[25]

Yet, in classic Madeleine style, the same object a prospective buyer had been refused for years, she would sell in a heartbeat to a child who found the object beautiful.

While Madeleine often demanded exorbitant prices for what other dealers might jealously term her "flea-market finds," she was an excellent negotiator when it came to her own buying. She was capable of visiting a piece in a colleague's shop for months until they came down to her lowball offer. The seller might have to await an equal number of months for payment, as Madeleine parted with money begrudgingly. In the instance when she found the item had been sold since her last

An impromptu wreath of berry branches imbued a biscuit porcelain figure grouping with romance and narrative.

visit, she would be furious as in her mind it was already hers. Conversely (and by her own account), if something pleased her, she might pay handsomely for it. She told the story of how a dealer whose wares she was browsing told her to make up her mind quickly because he had heard Madeleine Castaing was in the area.[26]

Madeleine loved the hunt. Flea markets were particularly thrilling as one never knew what one might uncover. Auction houses and other dealers' establishments, such as the antiquaire Hagnauer who was around the corner on the rue de Seine, were other favorite haunts. When something caught her eye, it was a heartpounding moment: "It's a big moment and there's a lot of emotion. But before anything there's the discovery, the object that lures me, that lures me to the point that I buy it. And right away I know what should surround that object. Right away it creates its own atmosphere."[27]

As Madeleine wasn't by nature a shopkeeper and preferred to be out looking for the perfect opaline *bibelot* instead of strapped down watching the till, it was necessary to have assistance. Jacques Damiot who was by her side in the very beginning had stayed with her at the opening of the Cherche-Midi boutique, but eventually tired of being in her shadow. His place was soon filled by Madame Crucifix who was hired on the spot and asked to start working that very minute so Madeleine could run errands.

"She was an ugly little woman but elegant, and she was wearing enormous glasses that made her look like an adorable owl. Brought up in the Jardin des Plantes, where her father was the longtime director, she had married Crucifix, the port heir, and then the family lost its fortune and they had to get jobs to provide for themselves. Madame Castaing adored her because she was cultivated, witty and she recited poems to her, but her choice could be surprising. . . . She was completely blind in one eye and the other didn't work very well so that when she was alone in the boutique, dishonest clients stole *bibelots*," recalled Laure Lombardini,[28] who came to Madeleine's shop as an intern in 1957 and stayed on for nearly fifty years, until 2004, when she was directing the shop after Madeleine's death.

Laure (a name Madeleine thought held more allure than Lea, her given name) was also originally from the Chartres area and had attended the same convent school as Madeleine. Her dexterity with a needle was taken full advantage of by Madeleine. Paulette Glinshe, who worked for Madeleine as secretary beginning in the 1950s until she opened her own shop in 1972, remembered, "The boutique's atmosphere was both romantic and unpredictable at the same time,"[29] marveling at the host of glitterati from the worlds of film, literature, and art who were clients and friends. A young Jean-Paul Riccardi urged Jacques Granges to secure him an internship with the fabled Mme Castaing and assisted her for a few years. His interior design work bears the unmistakable

Opposite: A cotillion of the Napoleon III and Victorian low-slung tufted chairs favored by Madeleine took up residence in one of her storerooms; Following: Madeleine on the prowl at a flea market in the 1960s.

Madeleine had several storerooms in the St. Germain neighborhood. This one on the rue Visconti was imagined as a winter garden.

In the same storeroom under the colonnade, floral chintz formed a tented enclosure. Bamboo furniture contributed to the sense of exoticism.

influence of *le style* Castaing. "She taught me the importance of being original, not simply remaking what others have done before. Rooms should not only be poetic but terribly personal."[30] This ethos perhaps explains how many tried to copy her distinctive style, but have never fully captured the same esprit.

Other support staff included Paul de Saint-Sauveur, an penurious but proud count who worked as her accountant; Joseph Boudon, a handyman who ran errands and performed other small chores, replaced in 1979 by the able Mamadou until the shop closed its doors in 2004. Madeleine, who always had a penchant for the eccentric over the conventional, had a terse Russian alcoholic as maître d'hôtel succeeded by the charming Amido, a Moroccan drag queen by night and white-gloved, impeccable majordomo by day.[31]

A STYLE MATURES

Soon after the shop opened, Madeleine and Marcellin moved from their rue d'Aumale apartment to live on the entresol above. Small and intimate, the space was comprised of a low-ceilinged bedroom and sitting room whose windows looked out onto the traffic lights of the rues Jacob and Bonaparte. The flora-and-fauna patterened carpeting and curtains used throughout the entresol undoubtedly quelled the din of the street and provided the couple with a verdant retreat in the heart of the city. Its small windows were an advantage: Madeleine preferred the atmospheric result of pools of light thrown from lamps to the brilliant glare of the sun. After Marcellin's death in October 1966 from a heart attack, Madeleine couldn't bear to live in the space and soon moved upstairs to an apartment directly overhead. Its front door was just feet away from that of another legend of design, the modernist Eileen Gray, who had been living there as a recluse since the 1920s. Here Madeleine installed many of her favorite Soutines in rooms whose decoration benefited from the decades of experimenting and defining her style, with only exception being the kitchen–kitchens in general held no interest for her. More than any of her other interiors, here and at Lèves was where her style was at its most personal and pure.

An enfilade of three reception rooms ran along one side of the apartment parallel to a gallery. As at Lèves, it was fully furnished with banquettes, bookshelves, and console tables. In the dining room, with its perpetually set table, one found the perfect example of stagecraft. Under the porcelain service, mother-of-pearl-handled flatware and white draped cloth sat not an antique mahogany table, but sawhorses!

From the relatively unlayered dining room which brings Josephine's restrained elegance to

Opposite: Even though Madeleine and Marcellin's entresol apartment was small, ample space was designated for a dressing room where her extensive collection of hats that could be carefully stored; Following: In the entresol bedroom, the formal elegance of the Neoclassical mixed with the cozy eclecticism of the mid-nineteenth century, resulted in a cocktail that is classic Castaing.

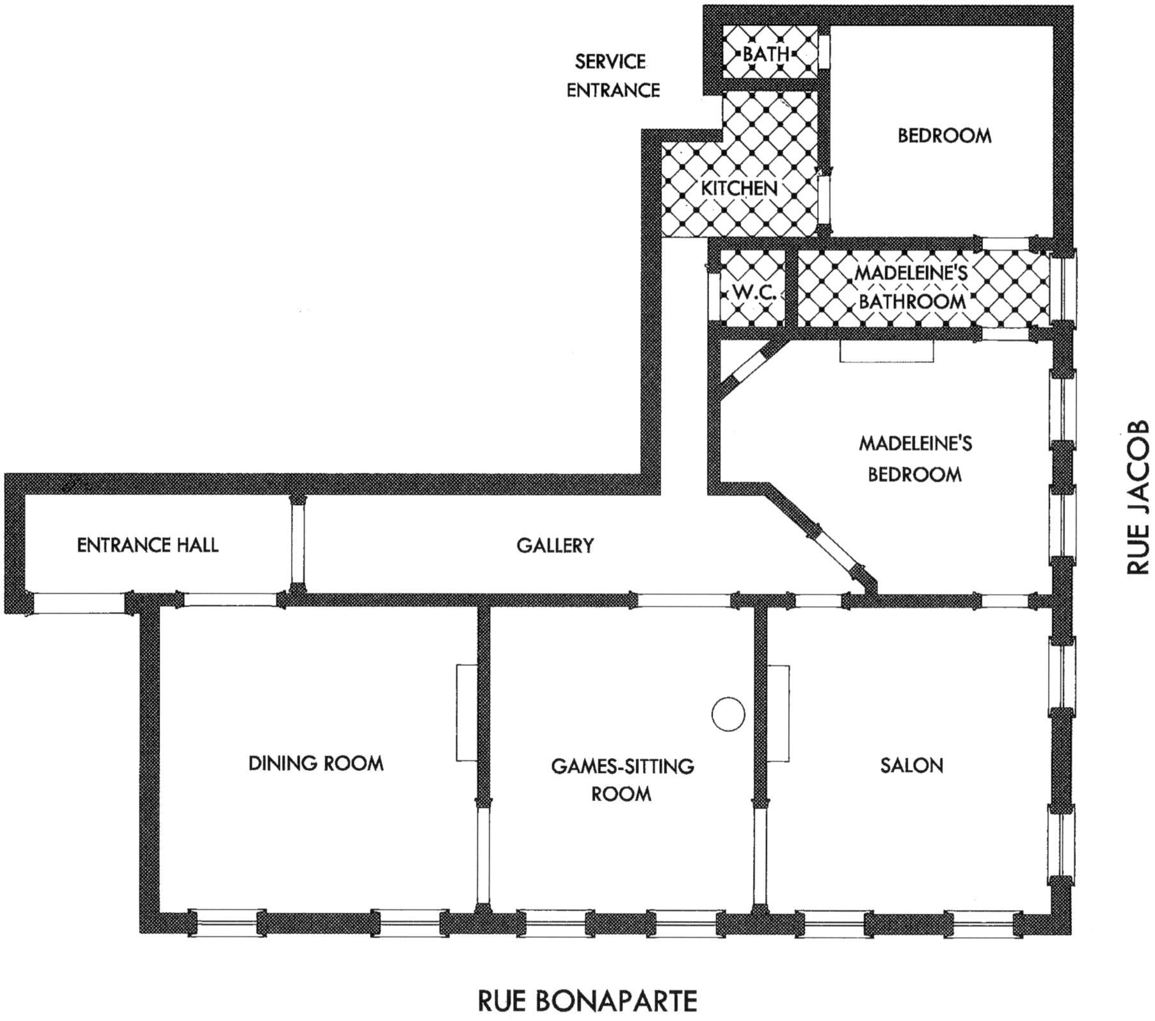

SERVICE
ENTRANCE

BATH

BEDROOM

KITCHEN

W.C.

MADELEINE'S
BATHROOM

MADELEINE'S
BEDROOM

ENTRANCE HALL

GALLERY

DINING ROOM

GAMES-SITTING
ROOM

SALON

RUE JACOB

RUE BONAPARTE

Two spreads preceding: The salon of the entresol was originally furnished as a cocoon for the devoted couple. Only the chosen few were asked upstairs to tea; Preceding spread: Carpeted in "Carrelage Castaing" and painted a flattering rosy pink, the entresol bathroom was a room to linger and relax in; Above: The floor plan of the first floor apartment directly over the shop which Madeleine purchased after Marcellin's death in the 1960s.

The gallery looking toward the entrance hall was furnished with banquettes and bookcases and as layered a space as any of her other rooms. The view onto a courtyard was shielded by the nineteenth-century hand-painted roller shades Madeleine was keen on.

Even a narrow corridor, which continued from the gallery to the kitchen, was an opportunity for fantasy and invention. Here Madeleine channeled the exoticism of the Regency's Brighton Pavilion for this bamboo-trellised passageway.

The only room Madeleine had little interest in was the kitchen, which was simply decorated in black and white and of small scale; Following: The dining room table was perpetually set with a Napoleon III table-fountain festooned with faux ivy taking center stage.

Preceding: Cobalt blue dazzled the eye in the games room and occasioned it to be dubbed the "salon bleu." A Directoire billiard lamp with blue tole shades was the inspiration for the room's décor; Above: An enfilade of doors connected the dining room, games room, and grand salon along the rue Bonaparte.

When upholsterers were preparing the walls of the games room for fabric, Madeleine was so charmed by the white flannel underpinning that she stopped them from proceeding. Instead broad blue ribbon banding provided the finishing touch.

mind, one continued down the enfilade to an adjacent games room which was chock-a-block with tables and chairs. Both in this room and the dining room, Madeleine wittily upholstered the walls in white flannel batting. Her original intention had been to upholster th walls as in the salon, but before the final silk or cotton could be hung, Madeleine was so charmed by the effect of the under layer of batting, that she decided to leave it. Wide navy blue ribbon banding provided the finishing touch. A large Directoire billiard lamp, similar to one at Malmaison, was the starting point for the room and hung above a pair of green baize-lined games tables, each supporting a figure of a Viennese porcelain swan. Here were placed her favorite chair which she claimed belonged to Josephine herself and a white porcelain stove, a Castaing trademark.

Off of the blue and white striped salon was her bedroom. Like the Summer bedroom at Lèves, it is furnished in pinks and whites, like the inside of a "shell, like that from which Venus rose out of the sea," punctuated by gilt bamboo furniture. Just as Balzac's De Marsay "experienced one of those delicate sensations which true poetry gives" upon entering the boudoir of *La Fille aux yeux d'or*, so too did any visitor to Madeleine's private sanctuary.

Opposite and above: Sumptuous yellow taffeta curtains complement the myriad blues which dominated the grand salon. Madeleine installed many of her favorite Soutines from Lèves in the apartment, such as *La Femme au bain* hanging over the Regency painted settee (opposite).

The guiding influence of Neoclassical architecture is readily apparent in Madeleine's bathroom where even the bathtub is set within a coffered Roman arch;
Opposite: Close friend François-Marie Banier, Harold to Madeleine's Maude, scrawled "Où vas-tu Bellissima?" on the mirror in Madeleine's bedroom.

Following: Numerous chairs and chaise longues created several conversation corners. The paneled doors were painted with "cloud" decoration inspired by the blooms of water stains on the wallpaper.

A nineteenth-century giltwood console table served as a writing/dressing table. Photographs of family and friends spanning several decades flanked by two pink opaline oil lamps covered its surface.

A gilt-bronze faux bamboo vitrine purported to have belonged to Napoleon III's sister enclosed several figurines of maidens in a state of undress.

LE STYLE MALMAISON

*"…I love Malmaison; it's a wonderful house
where you feel like living, laughing, blossoming."* [1]

MADELEINE CASTAING

World War II left France plundered both physically and spiritually. If its historic monuments and sites fared better than those of others from the onslaught of war, its pride and confidence were in shambles. A collective romanticized return to the country's glory days helped balm the wounds and bolster morale. This nostalgia was never more apparent than at home where modernist design was in the main eschewed for classical décor.

In her introduction to the 1960 book *Les Réussites de la décoration française* which illustrated some of the most exclusive residences of the day, Solange d'Ayen noted that most of the owners profiled had turned to traditional styles for both psychological *and* practical reasons: At the end of the war, it was public buildings, such as hospitals and schools, which received top-priority for rebuilding, not private residences. Furthermore, if something was added or modified to the private homes that did require attention during and immediately after the years of war, it was guided by the style of the preexisting structure. The prevailing wisdom was traditional architecture called for traditional furnishings.

D'Ayen's position as fashion editor of French *Vogue* as well as a duchess placed her as a peer to the illustrious style-setters and doyennes, including Madeleine and her clients, featured in the book and hence qualifies her words to reflect the general mood of her milieu. "The house became a sort of symbol of everything we were hoping for. A wave of tenderness enveloped these possessions, valuable to us both monetarily and sentimentally, keepsakes, treasures that were saved from the debacle. The idea was to have something new but familiar."[2]

Five years later, *Maison et Jardin* followed up with another compendium book, *Les Nouvelles Réussites de la décoration française*. The magazine's editor Thomas Kernan noted that although the country had enjoyed tremendous success during this period, no new blossoming of the arts had coincided. No *"style Charles XI,"* no new Matisses—instead an appreciation for the past continued to dominate interior decoration: "a synthesis of interior styles, drawn from the repertory of the past three hundred years" is the rule; at home, "the Frenchman and even more the French woman have remained rigorously conservative.[3]

The enfilade in Madeleine's Paris apartment was punctuated by Neoclassical busts on pedestals and the stately profile of a Regency table's lion monopodium support. "Carrelage Castaing" carpet and "Dentelle" curtains were both inspired by Empire period document designs.

Madeleine's interiors were joined by those of Emilio Terry, Charles de Beistegui, Georges Geffroy, Victor Grandpierre, Gerard Mille, Maison Jansen, and other acclaimed decorators in the pages of these two books as well as in the leading shelter magazines of the day. Although each had his or her own approach—some more distinct than others—they were all translators of period styles and knew their eighteenth century styles backwards and forwards, creating sympathetic surroundings for the priceless collections of ancient families and newly minted fortunes. The "period room" in which an interior is conceived as a museumlike setting with everything correct and appropriate to one particular style were just as in evidence as rooms that mixed a profusion of styles so as to give the impression of the accretion of past generations.

France's dominance in setting the style and fashions has long been used as an instrument of power, propaganda, and enrichment by its rulers. Louis XIV first recognized how influential style could be and ingeniously used it as a tool of glorification. His successors continued to place great emphasis on nurturing the applied arts even after the revolution; when Napoleon assumed the mantle of leader, one of his first actions was the revitalization of the luxury trades from porcelain to silk. Napoleon understood two things: that France's identity had become inextricably linked with its reputation as a leader of fashion, and that its economy was just as tied to purveying its accoutrements. Furthermore, both needed boosting then just as they did after the two world wars.

Before the wars, designers, fed up with the pastiche of period styles of the nineteenth century, purposely set out to contrive a new style. After their experiments with Art Nouveau were a commercial failure, they looked back to Neoclassicism, the last true style, as a point of inspiration and departure. This resulted in what has since been termed Art Deco, after the landmark 1925 *Exposition internationale des arts décoratifs et industriels modernes* in Paris where the style, then in its full flower, was shown to great acclaim. Originators of the style such as Emile-Jacques Ruhlmann and Louis Süe looked to Neoclassical antecedents—from the delicate Louis XVI to the severe, archeological Empire periods[4]—and reimagined them into the sleek new style.

As the Art Deco style took shape in France before and during the two wars, a concurrent taste for Neoclassicism in its original form also took hold. Stephen Calloway has dubbed this the Malmaison style[5] after the country residence of Josephine which many consider the genesis of the Napoleonic Empire style.

What makes Malmaison stand out from Napoleon's official residences was its modest size

Decorator par excellence to the jet set Georges Geffroy curtained the bookcase and overmantel mirror suggestive of tenting in the double-height salon of Loel and Gloria Guinness on the avenue Matignon. Cooly elegant Neoclassical furniture continued the high style note.

which translated into more intimate and informal spaces, less beholden to the demands of pomp and ceremony. More than any other place, it is where Napoleon's consort Josephine felt most happy and at home, and where her renowned taste most made its mark. In a society that was quick to castigate, Josephine's taste was applauded from all quarters; Mme de la Tour du Pin, who like Josephine was a rare survivor of the *ancien régime* and not prone to hyperbole, wrote of her Tuileries apartments: "[they] had been entirely refurbished as if by enchantment."[6] Josephine cherry-picked the architects Charles Percier and François-Léonard Fontaine to carry out the house's refurbishment and decoration under her close watch.

Percier and Fontaine, who were subsequently appointed Napoleon's imperial architects, disseminated the formal, weighty Empire style which took the form and decoration of the ancient Roman empire as its inspiration. The team deepened their understanding of classical design by studying antiquities firsthand in Rome. Upon returning to Paris, they designed sets for the theater, which honed their abilities to create dramatic and spectacular designs. It is most important to note that Percier and Fontaine were given very short amounts of time to realize the opulent schemes that befitted Napoleon's ambitions. Their experience with the secrets of theater served them well, and they created striking and instantaneous effects with draping, passementerie, and flat painting.

The Malmaison style had an evident chic and a graphic quality that made it dramatic and self-conscious. Strong symmetrical Neoclassical architecture, a lack of clutter, contrasting colors and borders, and rectilinear furniture forms were characteristics embraced by the revivalists. Tented rooms, often of striped material, recalling Napoleon's Council Room, were embraced for a dash of pomp and panache. Simple curtains, often with pinch pleats, were most common and used liberally for windows as well as portieres, connecting back to the tented look. Josephine herself had a penchant for tents and took any opportunity she could to incorporate them into her design schemes. Even the very entrance to Malmaison was a tent, which as scholar Eleanor DeLorme points out, went against any sense of protocol.[7]

On her visits to Napoleon on campaign, Josephine was taken by the tents made of striped ticking. The emperor's own tents were always blue and white striped, and his consort was known to have bought huge quantities of the material. At the smallest opportunity, Josephine would order makeshift tented shelters for outdoor entertainment or refreshments, but most notably this great lady of style and imagination didn't limit herself to the out-of-doors. Napoleon's Council Room at Malmaison was modeled after a military tent on a lavish scale and received great acclaim. The tented room was imitated by many then as well as in the twentieth century. However, Josephine didn't stop with the Council Room and relegate tenting to masculine spaces—she also tented her

Opposite: Madeleine tented the entrance to Mireille Fellous's flat with blue-striped cloth similar to that used by Napoleon while on campaign. The grass-patterned carpet whimsically suggested one was in a forest encampment; Following: Josephine's love of tenting was expressed in her bedroom at Malmaison with giltwood poles and raspberry red silk hangings.

Left bank antiques dealer and decorator Raoul Guiraud was one of the most prominent followers of the *le goût anglais* craze Madeleine initiated.
In this dining room, Guiraud embraced the Regency's theatrical tendencies.

Jansen, led by its head designer Stéphane Boudin, was one of the most illustrious decorating firms of the period. Its exclusive clientele from captains of industry to crowned heads hired them for their impeccable classical taste, as evidenced by this circular dining room in the Empire style.

dressing rooms and bedrooms, including her state bedroom at Malmaison, designed by Louis-Martin Berthault after her divorce.

Napoleon often chastised Josephine for her outrageous bills for passementerie. According to DeLorme, she promised her upholsterer an extra 10,000 francs if he would keep it "simple"! This understanding of the elegance of showing restraint instead of ostentation—an almost reverse snobbery—was another point on which Josephine attracted her admirers.

In 1904, banker turned philanthropist Daniel Osiris Iffla donated Malmaison to the state, which opened it as a museum two years later. Inside the public was delighted by the high-style interiors which incorporated tented rooms, mahogany furniture with rectilinear lines, rich colors such as tangerine and raspberry that offset the austere elegance of the classical *objets* and furniture forms, simple curtains, exquisite woven silks, and bold contrasting borders and painted decoration that reinforced the architecture.

A Directoire revival was in the air by the end of that decade and into the next. Leading couturier Paul Poiret featured Empire-waisted dresses set amidst Directoire furnishings in 1908 pochoir prints illustrated by Paul Iribe. The American playwright Edward Knoblock who did much to revitalize the Regency style (the Empire's British co-eval) was living in Paris at this time, and decorated his flat in the Palais-Royale in the Directoire style. Most likely it was exposure to this trend in Paris that fanned the flames to his later devotion to the Regency.

Besides being the last fully realized style, Neoclassicism appealed on other levels to the early twentieth century: its severe straight lines and flat decoration gave it a theatrical flair—when living during heightened wartimes, drama is par for the course. Conversely, its lack of superfluous flourishes which are core to the earlier Baroque and Rococo styles was more in keeping with the serious times. Contemporary sourcebooks praised the Louis XVI style for its "purely French character" and noted that it "is very much in favor throughout the world today." The Empire style also got a stamp of approval and was being used by "today's decorators" with "exciting results."[8] An article written in 1956 elaborated, "The reserve, refinement, and manageable scale of Directoire furniture responds particularly to the demands of today. One can see a connection between these two times which, in many respects, have so many points in common."[9]

In the 1950s, Malmaison underwent a redecoration program which was discussed widely, bringing Josephine and her style to the forefront again. A 1955 interview in the magazine *Connaissance des arts* with Joseph Billiet, the curator in charge of the restoration, noted that all the wall lights, candelabra, and other fixtures had been fitted with candles: "Not only do these candles give more elegance to the lighting fixtures, but they lend the rooms an impression of being ready for a reception."[10] This observation is significant as it suggests that the curators tried to breathe life into

Mirrors, marble, and statuary lent grandeur to a small space in the entrance hall of Josephine's country residence Malmaison.

Madeleine loved stories, and many of her pieces came with romantic provenances attached. This armchair, one of Madeleine's favorites, was reputed to have been Josephine's. A porcelain swan, the cipher of the empress, is positioned fittingly nearby.

One from a pair of giltwood chaises purported to have belonged to Napoleon's sister, Pauline Borghese, once adorned the salon at Lèves, but later sat in the corner of Madeleine's shop.

the house and convey the feeling that its mistress had just stepped out or might return at any moment. This was not a sterile, embalmed approach, and it undoubtedly appealed to Madeleine who often created tableaux of playing cards or books scattered about to create the same effect of life. Madeleine was a tremendous admirer of Josephine and closely identified with her taste. "Simply to astonish is not nearly enough; you need life. Look at Malmaison. That is probably the most beautiful house of all, moreover it could have been mine; but beyond beauty, it retains the charm of Josephine who left her mark there."[11] Simple mousseline curtains, mahogany Neoclassical furniture, an appreciation for black as an accent color, a strong classically conceived architectural background, and a fine balance between the simple and the sumptuous, the serious and witty are all predilections Madeleine and Josephine shared.

Classical architecture stressing symmetry, proportion, and perspective was part of the Malmaison style. Decorator Gérard Mille espoused ordered space as one of his cardinal rules. Before taking any further steps, he first established the perspectives, created axes, and established symmetry whether this meant adding or tearing down existing elements.[12] The work of eighteenth-century architect Claude-Nicolas Ledoux held particular interest. Ledoux was one of France's earliest Neoclassical architects who was most associated with the *ancien régime*. The designs of Palladio were one of his primary sources of influence and simplified monumental forms typified his style. It was this simplification which was notable and influential to twentieth century French designers, just as the architect John Soane was to their British contemporaries.

It would be impossible to examine the Malmaison redux scene without a mention of the Lefuel family who were descendents of Hector Lefuel, architect to Napoleon III as well as of the Jacob family of ébénistes who for generations supplied furniture to the throne, including Napoleon. Their Paris residence in the 1950s was a pure expression of the Directoire style and a rare example of the museumlike approach to a period style, with every element from rugs to the Wedgewood-mounted doors sourced from another Empire-period *hôtel particulier* authentic to the early nineteenth century. However, over time the curatorial approach of the Lefuels became more rarified especially as the fully upholstered sofa and low table became essential items for a salon and instantly transported a room into the twentieth century. From the interwar period through the 1960s, an eclectic approach to mingling different period styles increasingly became the rule.

Two practitioners of *le style* Malmaison who most closely parallel Madeleine Castaing were Emilio Terry and Charles de Beistegui. Both were of foreign descent, independently wealthy, and had a highly developed interest in period styles. Both, interestingly enough, also purchased chateaux during or following World War II.

Emilio Terry was born Jose Emilio Terry y Dorticos in 1890 in Cuba. His family was of Hispano-

The Council Room at Malmaison was where Napoleon convened with his advisors. Its decoration was a high style translation of his quarters while on military campaign. The X-form stools recall the *sella curculis* used by the Ancient Romans to denote political power.

The apartment of Madame LeFuel was one of the most historically accurate recreations of the Empire period. Wedgwood decoration taken from an Empire period *hôtel particulier* was applied to the frieze of the yellow sienna walls and to the doors.

As descendants of the celebrated ébénistes Jacob, they had a singularly magnificent collection of furniture, which they took great pains to display.
This room in the LeFuel residence makes a clear reference to Napoleon's Council Room at Malmaison.

Irish descent and made its fortune in the Central Caracas sugar plantations. Terry fashioned himself an architect, and designed furniture, tapestries, interiors, and gardens for such clients as Greek-shipping magnate Stavros Niarchos, crowned Prince Rainier III of Monaco, and French blueblood and collector Charles de Noailles. While a child, Terry's family owned the mannerist Château de Chenonceau which had been remodeled for the royal mistress Diane de Poitiers in the sixteenth century and remains to this day one of the great castles of the Loire valley.

Terry lived in great style and his residences included a grand apartment in the eighteenth-century place du Palais-Bourbon and the Neoclassical Château de Rochecotte in the Loire Valley which he purchased in 1934 from his brother-in-law. Rochecotte, like Chenonceau, had a glorious history connected to the Duchesse de Dino, who was gifted the house in 1825 by her uncle, the noted diplomat Talleyrand. The duchesse—in tune with the romanticism of her time—made additions of columns, pergolas, and extensions to modify the chateau into an Italianate-style villa. Terry had a tremendous appreciation for Rochecotte's past and kept the Duchesse de Dino's furniture, rounding it out with sympathetic examples of the same period. Rochecotte's overlay of nineteenth-century revivalism onto Neoclassical architecture would have been a natural inspiration for the signature mélange of Napoleon III and Malmaison that Terry and de Beistegui played with and Madeleine made her own.

In the 1950s, Terry was hired by Charles de Beistegui, who was heir to a vast Mexican silver fortune, to decorate his newly acquired Château de Groussay. Beistegui was a professional man of style, but a professional decorator he was not or at least pretended not to be. De Beistegui's first notable adventure in decorating was for an apartment with a rooftop terrace on the Champs-Élysées for which he commissioned Le Corbusier in 1929 with the intent of fusing Le Corbusier's commitment to modern living with de Beistegui's interest in Surrealism. Presumably to Le Corbusier's horror, de Beistegui arranged Rococo revival furniture which made a perverse juxtaposition with the ultra-white modernist interior architecture.

De Beistegui, who liked to change things up and often, commented years later, "In 1929, my entire house was a bathroom. Now, my bathroom resembles a bedroom." By the 1950s, his interiors in town and in the country had evolved backwards in time. At Groussay, he favored a range of periods of the furniture, objets, and paintings, with the Louis XVI, Empire, and Charles X styles most in evidence. This catholic cocktail of styles aligned with his belief that interiors shouldn't be museum recreations of a particular moment as the whole idea of a period room is a fallacy as most rooms show the residue of different generations. As de Beistegui had very definite views of what he liked and even occasionally worked as a decorator for others, certain that Groussay was a collaborative effort.

Emilio Terry's bathroom in his Paris residence channeled the Directoire style with its careful use of Neoclassical elements. Dubbed the inventor of the Louis XVII–style, Terry saw himself as part of a long line of architects working in the classical tradition.

Millionaire aesthete Charles de Beistegui decorated his country house, the Château de Groussay, with the assistance of designer Emilio Terry, in his favorite Louis XVI and Empire styles. The Goya Gallery was pure pomp and pageantry.

The print rooms fashionable in eighteenth-century England inspired the decoration of this small dining room at Groussay. The coffered ceiling was after the designs of British Neoclassical architect Robert Adam and the "Louis XVII" mahogany console table was by Emilio Terry.

Terry and Madeleine both had an appreciation for the contrary and included off-kilter elements that transformed what might be traditional into surprising. François-Marie Banier remembers that Madeleine always had to have one strange object in a room: "If the object was awful, she put it completely in the middle to have the eyes turning around it."[13] Terry as a true designer was experimental with forms and could rework traditional inspirations into something completely novel and different, as with the eye-popping rug inspired by ancient Roman mosaics he created for the Raymond Guests.[14]

What the eye may not ascertain when looking at the work of de Beistegui, Terry, and Madeleine is how daring it would have seemed at the time. Over the Malmaison references that formed the foundation of their style was laid a layer of mid-nineteenth-century Napoleon III—considered by many to be the epitome of bad taste just as Victoriana is in Britain and the United States.

Reimagined in more contemporary colors—sometimes more shocking and sometimes more pretty—flowered carpets, fringed and tasseled upholstery, and extravagantly tufted furniture forms such as the tête-à-tête and slipper chairs were brought into the mix. When Banier explains that every style is developed as a reaction to an existing style, and that Madeleine's was against that of Maison Jansen who were renowned for their flawless historicism, he is referring to her embrace of the unfashionable mid-nineteenth century. Besides rebelling against conventional edicts of taste and therefore ironically being in the vanguard by looking to the past, these elements added an undeniable component of comfort—something that was essential to any Castaing space.

THE VOGUE FOR REGENCY

"When it comes to decoration, the marriage of English comfort with French taste is quite possibly the most important event of the mid-twentieth century."[15]

Madeleine was widely credited with bringing the English Regency style to Parisian salons,[16] and she often remarked that she was on the first boat to Dover at the end of World War II and came back with a truckload of finds: "I took the first peacetime ship in order to bring Sloane Street and Chelsea to Paris."[17] Interior design historian Mario Praz, who was also prowling around London antique shops for Regency furniture at the same time, noted how incredible finds could be had for

Emilio Terry boldly reimagined ancient mosaics for the black, white, and periwinkle blue rug in the otherwise very traditional living room in the Paris residence of Mr. and Mrs. Raymond Guest, née Princess Caroline Murat.

Esteemed antiquaire Jean-Philippe Hagnauer, from whom Madeleine made many purchases, decorated this double-height library with English Regency antiques and a cabbage-leaf carpet. The passementerie borders applied to the seat furniture cushions were a common Empire treatment.

Floral blossoms ran riot along the walls and floor of Vicomte Charles de Noailles's country house living room. Emilio Terry deftly used restrained Neoclassical furnishings to keep the mix from becoming too sweet.

The ivy-leaf carpet installed in the Rotunda Bedroom at Groussay hinted at Madeleine's involvement and in any case confirmed de Beistegui's like-minded appreciation for the mid-nineteenth century, a theme further developed by the suite of chintz-covered tufted chairs.

Madeleine's stand at the 1948 Salon des Antiquaires mixed elements from different periods and locales to evoke a past that never existed. Alexandre Serebriakoff, who painted both pictures on these pages, was a constant guest at Groussay and a frequent collaborator with Beistegui and Terry.

paultry sums as the style itself was not considered fashionable or important like the earlier Queen Anne or "Chippendale" styles.

Although the Regency style is contemporary with the French Empire, it was visibly distinguishable from its continental cousin. One tremendous difference between English and French interiors of the early nineteenth century was that the English had fallen into the custom of leaving their furniture in the middle of the room, instead of dragging it back to the wall when it was no longer in use. Small-scale tables, chairs, and other pieces of furniture were made to float in the center of rooms and were affixed with castors to be more easily pushed and pulled around. Regency furniture also avoided of the ponderous heaviness of the Empire that Madeleine so abhorred.

The British fascination with the exotic played out in rare timbers and orientalizing decoration. While many peers of the realm experimented with pan-Asian motifs and forms, the Prince Regent took it to another level at his Royal Pavilion in the seaside resort of Brighton. Madeleine is reputed to have visited Brighton, one of the most exuberant and fanciful displays of this trend, and to have been very much taken with its fantasy and whimsy. Bamboo was a constant motif in her work and perhaps seeing it at the pavilion incorporated into furniture and trompe l'oeil wall decoration informed this preference.

As she turned her shop into a "minimanoir de Sussex,"[18] *le tout* Paris took notice and Anglomania became de rigueur. Christian "Bébé" Bérard, who stood at the epicenter of high art, high fashion, and high society was instrumental in bringing the right people to her shop when it first opened. He became so enthralled by the English craze that he upholstered his own bedroom in a red and pink striped fabric copied from the walls of the Covent Garden opera house entrance hall. By the early 1950s, advertisements for other Parisian dealers specializing in "Sheraton" and Regency abounded in the back of decorating magazines.

In 1959 English design was deemed of significant enough interest to result in the production of *Le Style anglais: 1750-1850*, the last in a series on French design history published by *Connaissance des arts*. The editors noted, "Thanks to the craze for English Regency furnishings that broke out not only in France but all over the world, for several years we have seen the birth and growth of a new and legitimate curiosity for all artwork that came from England."[19] Three reasons are enumerated by the editors as to why the French became so enchanted: first, the Regency's simplicity, delicacy, and petite proportions were easy to place in small apartments; it mixed just as easily with modern as it did with antique furniture; and finally, "*l'argument decisive*," no matter how superb the quality, the prices were well below those for French eighteenth-century furniture. Appropriately, Madeleine had several rooms featured in the book. "Romantic, fanciful, picturesque, a bit theatrical" is the description of English style,[20] but it could equally be applied to *le style* Castaing.

Opposite: Madeleine posing next to one of the gilt-brass bamboo stands, which were always stocked in her boutique; Following: Bébé Berard, who got swept up in the neo-Regency craze introduced by Madeleine, covered his bedroom walls in a pink and red stripe copied from the entrance of the Covent Garden Opera House in London.

The dining room in Madeleine's Paris apartment was furnished almost completely with Regency furniture. Even the tablecloth was draped exactly as the Prince Regent's was at his splendid pleasure palace, the Royal Pavilion in Brighton.

Zuber's 1849 "Eldorado" panoramic wallpaper transformed this dining room by Raoul Guiraud into an earthly paradise.

A UNIVERSE "COCTEAU CASTAING"

"…where the disorder from outside and the drama of the world demand a refuge padded with books and with objects that are mysterious because they're forced to live far away from where they came." [1]

JEAN COCTEAU, "*Décor d'une jeune fille*" (1961)

By the 1950s, Madeleine had become one of France's most sought after decorators. Her eccentric fairy-tale settings resonated profoundly with a country that had seen the horrors of war and was treating its wounds with strong doses of nostalgia. Timing and talent played as much a part in her stratospheric rise as did the patronage of her first clients.

Bébé Bérard, who in his bearded person represented the convergence of art, fashion, and high society, was incredibly important in branding Madeleine's shop. His sometimes collaborator and equal at fusing the worlds of art and style was Jean Cocteau. The avant-garde poet-cum-artist was even more pivotal in the initial shaping of Madeleine's reputation.

Cocteau and Castaing first crossed paths in the 1920s through Madeleine's younger brother Gérard. Gérard and his close friend Jacques Guérin were at this time deeply enamored of the Frivolous Prince and part of the coterie of young homosexual men that encircled him.[2] Many artists and writers, including Madeleine's close friend Maurice Sachs who once worked as Cocteau's secretary, castigated Cocteau for his tendencies to pursue fashion and fame. Cocteau, for his own part, was unapologetic: "To live on earth, you must follow fashion, even when your heart isn't in it."

Cocteau may have been easily impressed by aristocratic pedigrees or the brightness of celebrity, but when it came to valuing talent, he didn't discriminate between the perfect simplicity of a dress by Chanel or an oil by Picasso. His lack of snobbery included embracing the forum of cinema as well as the more established vehicles of theater and the printed word, and utilizing humble materials such as shells, plaster, or straw whose primitiveness gave his work sophistication.

Jean Cocteau in the sitting room of his patroness Francine Weisweiller's Saint Jean-Cap-Ferrat villa Santo-Sospir. In the spring of 1950, he began to paint the interior of the villa with his favorite Greek mythological subjects.

Years before Cocteau gave Madeleine carte blanche to decorate his country house Milly-la-Forêt, furnishings from her store were used in several films with which he was involved. The first was *Les Dames du Bois de Boulogne*, a tale of scorned love based on a Denis Diderot novel and written and directed by auteur Robert Bresson with additional dialogue from Cocteau. Filmed immediately after the war and released in 1945, the film is imbued with austere glamour. The deadly Helene, played by Maria Casarès who also appeared in Cocteau's Orpheus trilogy, is the epitome of sophisticated elegance. Dressed in Grecian Madame Grès designs, she lives in an apartment equipped with tell-tale Castaing signatures from a black lacquer Regency work table to the mantel dressed with mirrored obelisks marred by large blooms of oxidization. A deer antler chandelier incongruously hanging in a bedroom whose prettiness underscores Elina Labourdette's blanc-mange bride is a signature example of Castaing perversity.

A few years later, Cocteau entrusted the art direction of *L'aigle à deux têtes* to Bérard who had already worked on the production design of Cocteau's *La Belle et la bête* to spectacular results. This out-of-time, out-of-place fairytale was set in a romantic Baroque castle, a perfect setting for Madeleine's whimsy. Its lead was played by the square-jawed, square-shouldered Jean Marais, a longtime favorite of Cocteau's. Marais became an habitué of Madeleine's shop and joined the list of those who pleaded with her to sell them that chair or this vase.

Cocteau's chief benefactress was Francine Weisweiller, a socialite hailing from an old Jewish banking family married to an American millionaire. It was a close, loving friendship that came with benefits: Cocteau found financial security for the last thirteen years of his life while Francine gained access to some of the most dazzling minds and creative talents of the time while her husband Alec was off with his horses or mistress, the film star Simone Simon. They first met in 1949 when Weisweiller's cousin Nicole de Rothschild was engaged to act (under the name Nicole Stéphane) in the film version of Cocteau's *Les Enfants terribles*. Weisweiller generously agreed to let scenes be shot in her magnificent *hôtel particulier* at 4, Place des Etats-Unis which she shared with her husband and young daughter Carole.

It was the Weisweillers who gave Madeleine her first major commissions. In addition to the Paris residence, Madeleine decorated their country house in Mortefontaine and their villa, Santo-Sospir, in Saint-Jean-Cap-Ferrat. After the splash Madeleine's shop made, it was only a matter of time before *le tout* Paris asked Madeleine to wave her magic wand in their own homes. She couldn't have dreamed up more perfect first clients: wildly rich, glamorous, and possessing a deep sympathy for Madeleine's unconventional style.

Francine first came across *le style* Castaing at the Cherche-Midi shop. A porcelain service decorated with ivy displayed in the window caught her eye and when she asked to purchase it, she

Opposite top: Actress María Casares plots her revenge against an ex-lover in Robert Bresson's 1945 film *Les Dames du Bois de Boulogne*. Props from Madeleine's shop furnished the villainess' icily elegant flat; Opposite bottom: Madeleine's eclectic mixture of periods and provenance was perfect for the fairy tale castle in *L'aigle à deux têtes*, based on the play by Cocteau with set decoration by Bébé Bérard.

A fierce buffalo horn armchair surprised visitors in the ultramarine blue marble entrance hall of Cocteau muse Jean Marais's country house. Even though Marais decorated his newly built house himself, he was an habitué of Madeleine's shop where horn furniture was often stocked.

Marais made most of his purchases from the decorator-dealer Hagnauer from whom Madeleine also shopped heavily. The blue silk upholstery and the Restauration period furnishings spoke to the indirect influence being in her sphere had.

was refused. "My dear mother, single-minded as she was, tried ten times in a row, and Madeleine, weary from the war, finally agreed to sell her the ivy service for a small fortune," recalled Carole in her memoir, *Je l'appelais Monsieur Cocteau*.

Francine and Madeleine became great friends and in 1948 Madeleine undertook her first project for the Weisweillers: their Picardy country house in the rural locale of Mortefontaine. Set near the border of the Ermenonville forest, one of the traditional hunting grounds of the kings of France, the "Folie de Francine" was secluded by trees and fields.

Carole recalled of the remarkable house:

> From the front you came directly into the dining room by climbing up a double staircase that led to a little flight of steps covered with mauve wisteria. The carpet in the room, as an extension of the garden, was printed with leaves of all shades of green; the mahogany furniture and a shiny old copper dish warmer were of the purest Victorian style. Above the dish warmer, I remember a painting by Berthe Morisot of a woman and a child eating at the table . . . . The objects, the paintings, the sconces . . . they all evoked the forest and the animals that live there.[3]

As if Snow White in a Disney film, Carole imagined herself speaking to all the beasts of the forests who, in porcelain or bronze doré form, lived indoors with her: "Each time I got to Mortefontaine, I'd rush to see if the squirrel in relief on one of the pedestal tables, the fox on the vases, the deer chandeliers, or the leaf ashtrays nibbled at by porcelain insects were still in the same place."[4]

Alec had promised his wife that if they survived World War II, he would purchase the house of their dreams in the south of France. The villa of Santo-Sospir overlooks the bay of Villefranche, perched 150 serpentine stone steps up from the beach. In 1950, Cocteau with his lover and adopted son Edouard Dermit, known to friends as Doudou, came for their first visit. Immediately Cocteau set about "tattooing" the walls with his murals.[5] "Eight days after his arrival," Francine remembered, "he asked permission to paint an Apollo above the fireplace."[6] Soon, all the pristine white walls and ceilings were touched by Cocteau's brush. A tour of his handiwork was recorded in the 1952 short film *La Villa Santo-Sospir*. The villa was also the location for scenes from Cocteau's last film, *Le Testament d'Orphée*, which included a cameo role for Francine as *la dame qui s'étaient trompée d'époque* (the lady from another era) for which she wore a trailing white Balenciaga gown.[7] Cocteau instructed the designer that the dress should be "reminiscent of the canvasses of Claude Monet and the costumes of Sarah Bernhardt."

Of the three Weisweiller properties, Santo-Sospir was the most relaxed. "I didn't want to call in a fashionable designer to do it up, the way everybody else did in those days, so I took on the job of decorating it myself,"[8] explained Francine. Many pieces were purchased from Madeleine's shop and, as a frequent guest to the villa, she couldn't but help to have given Francine advice. This is an

Alec and Francine Weisweiller's country house in Mortefontaine was the first residence Madeleine decorated for one of her most important clients. A lively Indian floral fabric running riot through the sitting room was balanced by mahogany English Regency furniture.

instance, of which there must have been many, of Madeleine's influence as an inspiration as well as a source for furnishings without her taking on the official role of decorator.

A note of colonial luxe was struck throughout with black chintz printed with huge green leaves used for the salon's curtains and seat furniture. Two steps up was the dining room whose walls and ceiling were covered in woven wickerwork panels commonly used for garden fencing—a suggestion from Madeleine. Brightly painted Indonesian furniture, which Francine discovered at Madeleine's shop, enhanced the mood of exoticism. A vibrant tapestry of the slaying of Holofernes designed by Cocteau added to the surreal surroundings. Here, every morning, the Weisweiller-Cocteau ménage, including the young Carole, drank their ritual pre-breakfast cocktail, concocted of fruit juice, gin, Bacardi rum, with a splash of bitters.

The most formal of the Weisweiller residences was the *hôtel particulier* in Paris which had been built and inhabited continuously by Francine's mother's family except when seized by the Gestapo during the war. Across the illustrious square in number 11 lived Cocteau's earlier benefactress, Vicomtesse Marie-Laure de Noailles, in the mansion her grandfather Bischoffsheim had built. The jewelbox of the Weisweiller house was the boiseried salon on the second floor where one found the family's collection of priceless paintings signed by such masters as Delacroix, Corot, and Renoir, situated amongst fine eighteenth-century furniture, including examples by the noted ébéniste and distant cousin Adam Weisweiler. Carole recalled the scandal that ensued when her mother, at Madeleine's urging, installed in the middle of this "temple of the eighteenth century" a red velvet tufted "borne": "an unforgivable 'spelling mistake,' the symbol of the following century."[9]

After dinner, in the pearl grey silk dining room whose decoration had been entrusted (most likely by Alec) to the society architects Jacques and Henri Barroux, guests repaired to the bar on which Francine and Madeleine had gone to town. Carole remembered, "To get there, you'd go through a little room adjacent to the dining room and overlooking the garden called the *fumoir*, or smoking room. That spot, where you rarely lingered, was very charming, especially in the spring when the big chestnut tree branch, full of pink flowers, leaned tenderly over the balcony, filling the second-floor rooms with a lovely scent. The white silk on the walls and the black and copper of the furniture contrasted with the two couches covered in tiger velvet—which at the time seemed very nonconformist!"[10] But what most fascinated the young Carole was the head of a mouflon complete with horns, encrusted with cabochon-cut stones, and fitted for tobacco. Banana leaf–patterned carpet which continued along the hallway and staircase down to the bar helped complete the illusion of being in the wild.

The double-height bar, the most contemporary room in the house, featured an enormous L-shaped low slung sofa upholstered in buttery-soft black leather. A dramatic solution to filling the

In this sitting room Rattan furniture and a daring black-ground tropical chintz evoke French colonial elegance. Stacks of books, cushions, and flowers underscored the mood of casual comfort.

Just days after Cocteau first came to stay at Santo-Sospir, he started "tattooing" the walls. The Apollo over the fireplace was his foray into this wall decoration, soon to be joined by two fishermen on either side.

The dining room was where Madeleine most made her mark. The walls were ingeniously applied with woven wickerwork panels over which Cocteau's magnificent tapestry of Judith and Holofernes was hung.

Madeleine, however, did befriend the avant-garde composer of Gymnopédies which Madeleine wished to have played at her funeral. The scandal of *Parade*, whose orchestrations included parts for a typewriter, lottery wheel, and pistol, put Satie's name on the map at the age of fifty-one there.

"Painting was too forceful for this [decorating the walls]. I decided to set about things cautiously, drawing in such a way that strong strokes, seen from a distance, appeared delicate, like lines inscribed in an album."

soaring walls was to apply bamboo banding all the way up to and on the ceiling. No pictures were hung—the only artwork was a large drawing behind the bar itself. It was an angel bent over the program celebrating Cocteau's induction into the prestigious Académie Française done impromptu by the artist himself at the party following the ceremony. A piano, which no one except Cocteau knew how to play, was placed near the stairs.

Francine's bedroom, also entrusted to the Barroux brothers, was hung in deep red silk velvet. The white organdy hangings of the copper bed found chez Castaing added freshness to the opulent setting as did a floral needlepoint rug. In the adjacent boudoir, the Barroux were clearly put on the backburner as the caned tented treatment could only have been dreamt up by Madeleine. Dark rosewood furniture was met with a charming white faience mantelpiece embellished with sprays of blooms which appeared throughout the room in vases, on lamps, and elsewhere. Over time, the caned walls became increasingly obscured by drawings, paintings, and other personal mementoes she collected.

For Carole's sixteenth birthday, Madeleine was asked to redecorate her rooms occupying the whole of the third floor. "My bedroom became a bathroom and walk-in closet, pink and blue, with a sunken marble bathtub and white and blue stucco: a very 'Brighton Pavilion'–style décor. What was once the dining room when I was a little girl was turned into a bedroom with walls hung in ribbed red fabric. I'd sleep in an alcove enclosed with white embroidered organdy curtains printed with thick bands in the same red, black, and yellow as the draperies." Was it a coincidence that Madeleine used her "Rayure Cachemire" which had been inspired by a Russian shawl while Carole was in the middle of a Tolstoy phase? Cocteau didn't think so when he wrote: ". . . You think of Bakst's large-scale décor that Karsavina and Vaslav Nijinsky danced *Le Spectre de la Rose* in . . . ."[11] Carole remembered, "The copper fireplace and the little black (nineteenth-century English) furniture gave the room a very Proustian allure, said some of my mother's friends. I hadn't yet read Proust but thanks to that 'Cocteau Castaing' universe, I imagined what the Guermantes' house must have been like . . . ." She continued,

> My childhood playroom, which became a study, was transformed by Madeleine into a tent-lounge decorated in a matte silk printed with green foliage on a white background. On each side of the fireplace, two low black leather couches that matched the leather on the ceiling made the room very comfortable. Inspired by Milly [Cocteau's country house], on a black painted screen I had pinned up posters that my mother and the poet would bring me from the different exhibitions they went to.[12]

In 1946, Cocteau acquired his house in the sleepy town of Milly-la-Forêt located at the western end of the forest of Fontainebleau. After years of living in rented rooms, he was finally able to purchase a permanent retreat with the proceeds from his latest theatrical success, *L'aigle à deux têtes*. He lived in the stucco and brick seventeenth- century former bailiff's house complete with moat

Preceding: Francine posing in the fumoir of the Weisweiller's Paris *hôtel particulier*. The mouflon-head tobacco box enthralled Francine's daughter Carole; Opposite: In the corner of the fumoir, a staircase covered in the same banana leaf–patterned carpet descended to the bar.

Strips of bamboo applied to the walls and ceiling packed a graphic punch enhanced by the contrasting palette of deep red for the curtains, black leather for the banquette, and white-tiled floor in the double-height bar.

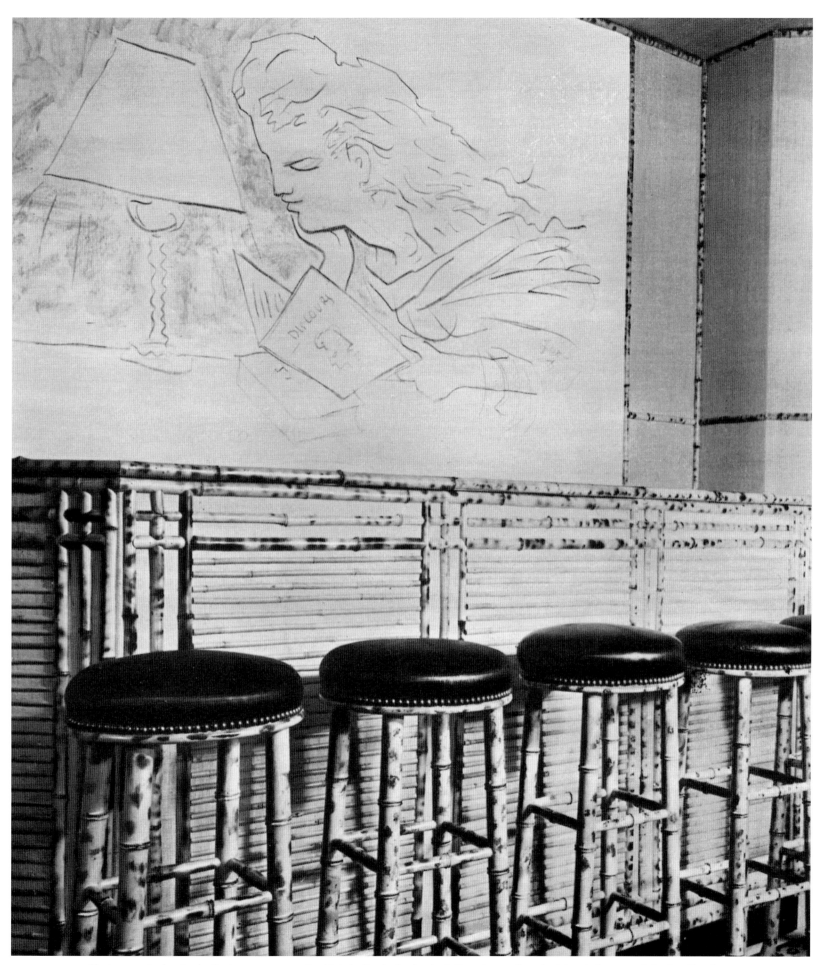

The impromptu drawing by Cocteau commemorating his induction to the Academie Française was the sole picture in the space; Following: Over time, the caned walls of Francine's boudoir became increasingly covered with watercolors, oils, and other souvenirs from her long patronage of the arts.

Many of the furnishings from the Weisweiller *hôtel particulier* have been reinstalled in Carole Weisweiller's current Paris residence, such as the black embroidered side chair which originally resided in Francine's boudoir.

The "winter garden" dining room which can be glimpsed through a doorway is classic Castaing, says Carole.

A simply furnished pale blue bedroom was perfect for a young Carole Weisweiller.

Upon her eighteenth birthday, several years later intense Russian red declared Carole's coming of age. Cocteau approved the décor and declared its calm and comfortable ambience full of books and mysterious objects a refuge from the drama and disarray of the world outside.

An entire floor of the Weisweiller Paris house was redecorated for Carole. As one magazine enthused, "the heart of this juvenile universe is the salon."
Tented with "Rayure Fleurie" like the Winter Bedroom at Lèves, it was filled with Carole's favorite things.

Posters from exhibitions Carole had visited adorned a folding screen behind the sofa. One of Cocteau's own filled with personal mementoes (following) was her inspiration. Black was used liberally, for the leather sofas, lamp shades, and elsewhere, as a counterpoint to the exuberant floral walls.

until his death in 1963. Madeleine was soon entrusted with the decoration, no doubt with Francine by her side plotting and planning away. A masculine setting was divined with jewel tones and mahogany furniture prevailing. Rattan, leopard print, and faux metal palms injected the same French colonial note found at Cocteau's other refuge, Santo-Sospir.

Just as at the villa, Cocteau put his own imprint on the house with his wall decorations and layers of personal souvenirs of lovers, friends, and pivotal events. In the library was a bust of a faun modeled after Marais, the only sculpture he ever made, which sat near a landscape painted by Marais with a putto mischievously drawn in by Cocteau. Francine recalled, "…Cocteau and I would shop for amusing or unusual objects. He had an eye for spotting oddities among secondhand dealers' bric-a-brac, and could transform them simply through the places he assigned them."[13]

For an artist who loved the limelight and whose life was perhaps his greatest work of all, it is notable that the house wasn't a stage set, but a sanctuary steeped in the memories and relationships of his life. For those curious as to why this personage whose career was set to the tides of fashion chose surroundings that were more traditional than of the moment may find their answer here: "'What are décors such as this good for?' ask depersonalized people. For nothing. For what the soul misses, for what it dreams of, for the diversion it seeks from the progress of unhappiness and from the inhuman reign of machines."[14]

Above and opposite: After years of living in hotels and rented rooms, the seventeenth-century Bailiff's House in the village of Milly-la-Forêt was Cocteau's first home. He wrote in *La Difficulté d'être:* "It is the house which awaited me. I live in this refuge, far from the bells of the Palais Royal…. The water of the moats and the sun on the walls of my room depict their unreal, moving surfaces. Spring is jubilant everywhere."

Snapshots of beloved friends and events were tucked into the wall dado trim amongst artfully arranged works by Renoir and Dufy.

In Cocteau's study, leopard print walls hinted at the exotic places Cocteau traveled in mind and spirit. A marble bust of Byron sat on a table beneath pinned-up photos of other male muses; Two following spreads: A leopard-patterned staircase and personal momentos on a mantel.

Top: Cocteau's bedroom, was kept exactly as it was during his life by adopted heir Edouard Dermit; Bottom and opposite: Even though the house's decoration was largely traditional, moments of wildness, such as a rooster figurine in the drawing room, remind one that its owner was an avant-garde poet.

Following: Rebelliously informal rattan chairs encircled the dining table stacked with a set of Cocteau-designed plates.

"Above all you have to love a house to make it a success; it's always a question of love. If you let your imagination go, your Heart, if you do away with the content, you immediately become a decorator."[1]

MADELEINE CASTAING

"Her houses are like mirror images. They are Narcissian and reflect those who are there."[2]

Film stars, potentates, princes, and literary luminaries all haunted Madeleine's fabled shop. Where else but chez Mme Castaing would one find New Wave director Roger Vadim with his latest flame while elegant lady of letters Louise de Vilmorin sipped tea? To become a client of Castaing was to enter a member's club as enchanted as it was exclusive. Once initiated, her disciples remained remarkably faithful: "For them, [what she said] was the gospel truth."[3]

Always the coquette, Madeleine compelled would-be buyers to pursue, plead, and seduce their way into their desired purchase. To buy even one item from Madeleine often took several visits to the shop; to become a regular customer could take Herculean amounts of patience, passion for *l'esprit* Castaing, and months, if not years. A genuine rapport was struck by the time one achieved habitué status, putting much credence in Madeleine's claim that she decorated only for friends:

> For me, a client is always a friend. Doesn't the mere fact that he comes into my shop prove that he has taste? When he comes in, I go towards him. I want to be friendly, to be useful to him. But I judge him. I follow his eyes. Are his eyes turning toward that dresser, toward that *bibelot*? I understand very quickly what he expects of me. So I take him into one of my rooms, we discuss literature, we reminisce. I absolutely need to understand his personality because I create "mirror" houses.[4]

Madeleine was generous with her advice, and her influence can be seen in rooms whose decoration she didn't professionally oversee. One glance at the salon of Louise de Vilmorin at Verrières

Madeleine in one of her signature fanciful hats while sitting on an American Federal four-poster bed dressed in snow white muslin and bobble fringe in an early incarnation of her and Marcellin's entresol bedroom.

is enough to be sure of Madeleine's guiding hand with its charming mix of chintz and fringe capped-off by a black-painted Napoleon III tête-à-tête. Letters to her friend, the penniless writer Violette Leduc, are full of advice on colors. In addition, there were certainly a number of faithful clients whose residences were filled with furniture and fabrics purchased from Madeleine directly, but who never hired her in an official capacity.

No records or archives exist to document the full breadth of client commissions. Although projects were published as early as the late 1940s and all the leading shelter magazines profiled her work right up until her death, there are tantalizing omissions of photographic records, such as the Swiss residence of the Prince Aly Khan or the Manhattan apartment of a Mrs. Peck. Many of her clients were as private as they were devoted, and there are several instances, according to her longtime assistant Laure Lombardini, of different generations continuing to work with Madeleine. Carole Weisweiller, the daughter of Madeleine's most important first client, continues to live with many of the items from her parents' residences which originated from Madeleine and gives great credit to Madeleine for awakening her eye and shaping her taste.

Before the poetry of decorating could begin, Madeleine first played the role of psychologist:

> I do a long psychological study. I live with the people who are entrusting me with their houses for two weeks. We eat together, we go to museums together, we take walks around Paris. And I talk to them a lot. They even talk to me about their lives. And I translate. I translate. Translation work, that's what I do. Their houses, their portraits. That's what you need. They give off a good feeling. No two houses look alike. But in each one, there's something in common. It's my style . . . my style. There's life, a lived-in feeling, but there's still a pursuit. There aren't any ugly objects. If an object isn't pretty, I put it in front as if it were an extraordinary wonder.[5]

One of the earliest records of a room by Madeleine is a dining room of the Victorian period that was part of "La Résidence Française" showhouse organized by *Art et industrie* magazine in 1947. The journal praised Madeleine for her "very confident taste, delightful creativeness, and a feeling for the local color."[6] The room is tented and outlined with a dark border—a technique Madeleine used for a Mme H. Ferenczi at the same time. Although the furniture—with the exception of the copper bar cart—is in the main English Regency, it is the cozy clutter of floral rugs, potted greenery, and *bibelots* that give the vignette its Victorian label. Interestingly, in the same showhouse, one decorator who dared to take Proust and the gilded Belle Époque as his inspiration was viciously attacked by critics. This vitriolic panning of nineteenth-century style references at the time helps in understanding how counter-current and rebellious Madeleine's own Balzacien point-of-view was.

The decorations for Mme Ferenczi and the anonymous "Mme D" are among the first client projects recorded.[7] Although signature elements are already in evidence, there are several choices

Madeleine's Victorian-themed dining room in the 1947 "La Residence Française" showhouse helped fuel the fashion for *le goût anglais*. Underneath the "cozy clutter" of the furnishing was an underpinning of Neoclassical architecture.

Madeleine created the perfect space for reading in a curtained alcove complete with bed and wallpaper panel of a verdant forest scene in a client's bedroom-library. A low mahogany fence contributes to the feeling of entering an encampment in the country.

The uncharacteristic elaborate curtains in this installation in Madeleine's shop betrayed her fascination at the time with Margaret Mitchell's novel *Gone with the Wind*. Madeleine identified strongly with its heroine Scarlett O'Hara's passion for Tara.

one doubts would have occurred ten years later when she was at her height, such as white walls, satin upholstery, and panoramic scenic wall paper.

Watercolors of the Ferenczi residence from 1948 give a rare snapshot of Madeleine's style at this early stage. The reappearance of items from the showhouse room such as the busts on brackets as well as the distinct bordered tenting used again in Mme Ferenczi's hallway make it tempting to conclude that the client asked Madeleine to recreate the room in her apartment. Here as with Mme D's residence, Madeleine is more restrained with colors and patterns. This restraint might be attributed to a (doubtful) lack of confidence in her own vision or to the more subdued tastes of the client, but what is most likely is that Madeleine was still experimenting and crystallizing what would become *le style* Castaing.

Without the benefit of knowing the client's directives and preferences, it is impossible to decipher how much of a free reign Madeleine was given. However, by comparing pictures of Madeleine's rooms for herself to those for her clients, one can see ideas and themes played out over and over again. The four poster mahogany bed dressed in shirred mousseline in Mme Ferenczi's bedroom was nearly identical to the one Madeleine had herself (and perhaps was even the same one sold to the client). In Madeleine and Marcellin's entresol bedroom at this time was an arrangement of several porcelain birds on brackets which is repeated in Mme D's dining room. Which was installed first? Did Madeleine choose the fabric for Mme Ferenzci's dining room curtains after or before she used it in her own at Lèves? It is impossible to ever know where an idea was first used, but what is clear is that once she deemed something to her taste, she used it again and again.

The consistency of the Castaing look was also reinforced by her faithfulness to the same stockists, manufacturers, and workrooms. Maison Hamot was her purveyor and fabricator for all her stuffs; Abat Jour Bouchardeau[8] supplied her lampshades—always of the same "coolie" style; from the early 1950s, Seigneur was her upholstery workroom who also made her simple pinch-pleat curtains. Roland Seigneur and his father both worked closely with Madeleine: "She was truly an artist. She knew exactly what she wanted. She had very strong opinions. You couldn't go against her wishes. Sometimes we went to the sites together to put things up; there's always a personal touch."[9] Many said of Madeleine that one never knew what she would do or say next. However, while she may have been spontaneous, she was also extremely loyal to her vendors, enjoying relationships with them for almost a half century.

For projects faraway, Madeleine didn't zoom back and forth—she merely composed the arrangements in her head and gave detailed instructions as to how all the components should be put together. The client then snapped a photograph to send back to Madeleine for her to judge the results full of mystery and life or to dispatch a new round of directions.

The entrance hall of Mme Ferenczi's residence superbly exemplified Madeleine's early work: a restrained use of color, a profusion of English Regency mahogany furniture, and a layout including several sitting areas.

It is impossible to miss the similarities between the dining room of "Mme D" photographed here in 1947 and the installation in Madeleine's shop, right, captured by watercolorist Alexandre Serebriakoff, at around the same time.

England, circa 1850, was the inspiration of the moment and one can see how Madeleine experimented with the theme in both of these rooms.

Examples of Madeleine's use of satin are scarce, and in general she stayed far away from shiny fabrics. Her own line included only one silk moiré. Here in Mme Ferenczi's bedroom, a Hollywood note of high fashion amped up the glamour.

When Madeleine liked something, she had no qualms about repeating it. Federal four poster beds simply dressed in white voile or muslin added an element of humble elegance in her own bedroom as well as in clients Mme Ferenczi's (opposite) and Francine Weisweiller's Paris residence.

To create an atmosphere, Madeleine paid close attention to details. In client Mireille Fellous's apartment, even the grey marble chimneypiece was monogrammed with its owner's initials.

Castaing blue, the color of opaline glass, trimmed in floral sprays infused Fellous's bedroom, photographed in 1957, with a fresh prettiness.

Another early client from this period was Jean Voilier, known more for her prodigious romantic conquests, both male and female, than for her writing or impressive business acumen as a director of two publishing houses. Who better to create a romantic lair for this blonde siren with the mesmerizing emerald eyes? The house itself was a former outbuilding to the Château de la Thuilerie and had been recently enlarged with an additional floor concealed by a mansard roof. The color selections were more bold: robin's egg blue and black carpeting in the dining room; azure walls and lemon yellow curtains with forest green carpeting in the salon; and patterns, including some which became part of the official Castaing line such as the carpet "Cachemire Castaing" in the library, appear in small doses.

The pièce de résistance, however, was the bedroom where many scenes of seduction transpired. Just as in the Summer Bedroom of Lèves, the walls were painted cherry red and overlaid with shirred white mousseline. The large copper bed was reputed to have come from the nineteenth-century military hero Patrice de MacMahon, created 1st Duc de Magenta by Napoleon III. Scarlet, black, and gold dominate the palette just as in the bedroom of Zola's courtesan Nana.

The apartment Madeleine decorated for the English-born composer Raphael Douglas, Baron von Banfield, better known by his stage name Raffaello de Banfield, is a prime example of her mature style. Banfield had studied at the National Conservatory in Paris in the late 1940s where he was introduced to Cocteau, Picasso, and other Paris art world heavies and it is easy to see how their paths would have converged. In this late 1950s project, her signature colors, fabrics, and carpets are all employed with classic Castaing chic. However, what is distinctive about this project is its clear masculinity. Key to achieving this was the strong Napoleonic architecture of moldings, arches, and colonettes brought in by Madeleine.[10] The Empire military theme was continued with the metal campaign-style bed and the salon's striped walls recalling the ticking used for campaign tents. A strong palette of azure blue for the salon and Madeleine's beloved Russian red enrobing the bedroom was chosen and set off by equally strapping pieces of Regency mahogany—a departure from the abundance of little tables and chairs usually found in a Castaing setting. The only feminine notes are the occasional arrangement of flowers and the ruby red ballroom gown curtains with swagged valance and ruffled edge which serve to soften and warm the room's Neoclassical reserve. Banfield was so thrilled with the apartment, he asked for a jacket and slippers to be made en suite with the bedroom wall hangings.[11]

When Nina Ricci, in her later years, and her husband Robert wanted to transform their Paris apartment into a retreat from the world, who better to turn to than Madeleine? Although modestly sized, the flat had a magnificent view overlooking the manicured greens of the Champs-de-Mars. For the living room which functioned as library, *fumoir*, and dining room, Madeleine delineated

In Jean Voilier's main sitting room, uncharacteristic strident swathes of color—including lapis lazuli, yellow, forest green, and garnet red—perhaps reflected the strong personality of its proprietress.

Madeleine used one of her signature carpets, "Cachemire Castaing," in black and green, in the library (opposite). Voilier's country house appeared in several magazines between the early fifties and sixties.

Madeleine set a tone of concentration and industry in Jean Voilier's library with a severe off-white and black palette with touches of green. Linen walls and shantung curtains in ecru contrast with black cut velvet upholstery.

Above and opposite: A children's treehouse of sorts provided guest quarters or the perfect place for an afternoon tryst. Two small rooms each furnished with a twin bed were raised on oak pillars and connected by a teak footbridge. In one, Madeleine's favorite print enveloped all.

Following: For Jean Voilier, who was more renowned for her romantic conquests than her literary endeavors, nothing less than a sumptuously sensuous bedroom would do. Just as in her own bedroom at Lèves, Madeleine layered white muslin over deep red walls.

Russian red and strong Neoclassical architectural elements, such as the ingenious arched niche which added storage space as well as visual interest, make composer Raffaelo de Banfield's bedroom an undeniably masculine domain.

De Banfield's piano takes center stage here with sweeping red taffeta ballroom curtains and a large scenic painting as a backdrop setting the scene for impromptu recitals; Following: Two maestros of arranging—one of music, the other of objects—collaborate euphoniously.

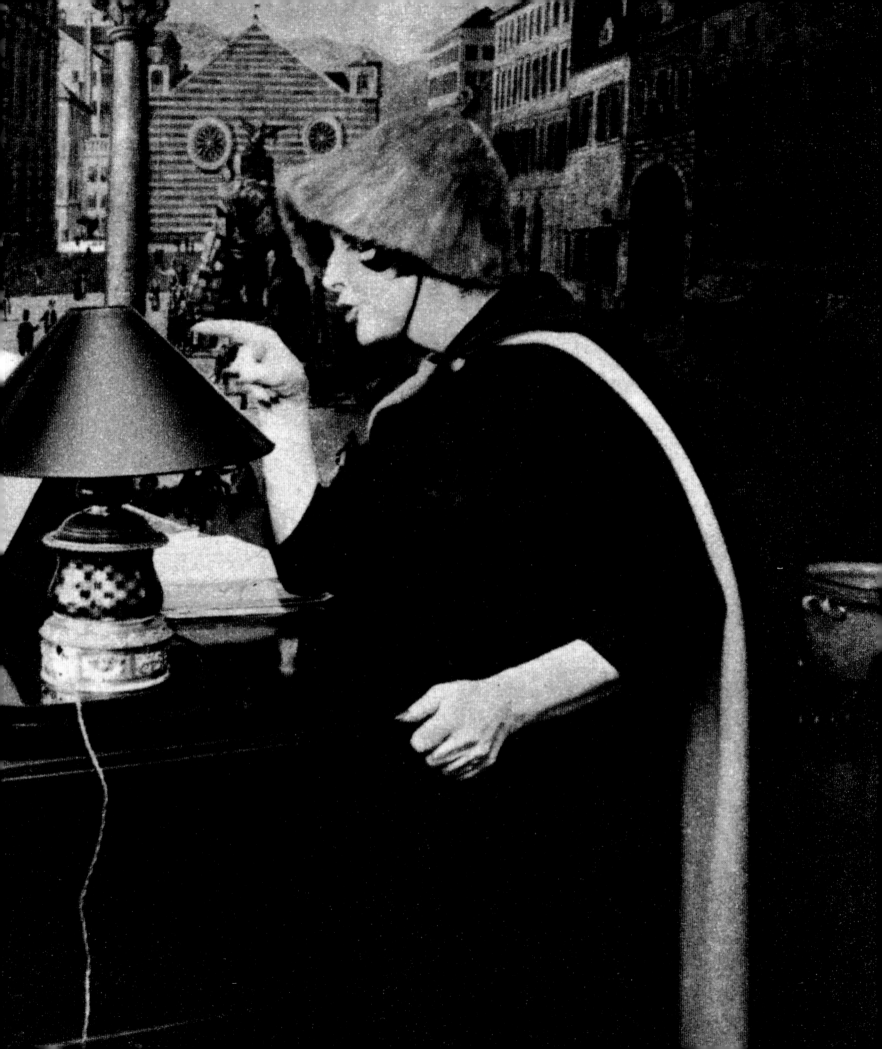

the space by creating corners. Other signature Castaing-isms abound: a favorite large scale floral cocooning the walls and windows of the living room; an entrance hall tented with painted stripes, and even a white porcelain stove in a contrived mirrored niche in Nina's bedroom.

However there are distinct variations—ones that beautifully suited a first couple of couture. In Robert's study, grey satin walls and white carpeting set off by a broad black border evoke Hollywood glamour. Pearl grey satin walls and "mouse" grey carpeting transported Nina's bedroom to the clouds, while blue and white candy-striped curtains and sofa hinted at the sky. Madeleine's uncharacteristic use of so much lustrous silk in the Ricci residence was clearly informed by the clients' fashion background.[12]

In 1964 at the second annual Salon des Antiquaires at the Grand Palais, Madeleine's undeniable impact on the world of design and decoration was paid tribute to by Minister of Culture André Malraux who proclaimed, "You honor France. Very fortunately, there are still people like you who know perfectly well how to express poetry." If she was a recognized figure then, it wouldn't be long before she was a national institution. She has been likened to Coco Chanel, and hailed, along with Jean-Michel Frank, as one of the two original French talents of decoration of the twentieth century.

It must be said that part of the public's fascination with her in later years wasn't just the look she created and branded, but the appearance of her own person. It was Marcellin's death in 1966 that prompted her to adopt the wig with elastic chin strap that have become so identified with her legend, taking her love of wearing whimsical hats in a new direction. "I wore them [elastic bands] all the time, all day long, but when Marcellin died, life was so hard. It was so difficult to start living again that I wanted to be a completely different thing, another woman."[13] Long false eyelashes, red lip-liner drawn well outside the lips, and a short dark brown wig underneath which was two centimeters of padding to augment her height transformed the septuagenarian's appearance. Her vanity was for her eyes only—she was well aware that others stared and mockingly referred to her as the "femme à l'élastique" but she famously retorted that when she looked in the mirror, she liked what she saw. And that was that. "In one month I begin my 90th year, but in actuality I believe that I'm 35 and I *am* 35!"[14]

All the same, when it came to divulging exactly how old she was, she was known to turn coy. In one instance, while purchasing a car, she put up a huge fuss when asked to show her identification card. When it was finally surrendered, the seller found a big blur over her date of birth.[15]

Even in her eighties, Madeleine still took on the occasional decorating project. In 1975, the magazine *Art et décoration* featured what must have been one of her last extensive commissions. While one imagines watching television would have been anathema to the literary-minded Madeleine, for this client on the Boulevard Suchet, she even went so far as to recess one into a wall. Two apartments combined into one opened out onto a private garden accessed by large floor-to-ceiling

Opposite: Madeleine always took great pains with her appearance, pleasing herself first and foremost. In her years post-Marcellin, exaggerated red lips, false eyelashes, and the famous wig with an elastic chin strap made up her signature look; Following: Madeleine continued Nina and Robert Ricci's view of the Champ-de-Mars with a lively floral print.

sliding doors which ran along the length of the apartment. Light and views of verdant flora and fauna, including magnolias and white rose bushes, infused the apartment. Who else but Madeleine could transport this Parisian apartment hectares away into the country? A grass green carpet of flowers and leaves covered the floor of the entrance, which was dramatically tented in red with "Rayure Cachemire" trim, and continued into the salon-cum-library. As at Lèves, a large *indiscret*, upholstered in the same foliate pattern to surreal effect, divided the two spaces. Blue and white striped upholstered walls suggested the room as a forest encampment.

Down below in the basement was the only room that seems clearly datable to the 1970s and as such, atypical of Castaing's canon. Neither red, blue nor green—her self-professed color lexicon—appear; instead a bright pumpkin orange electrified the room made further wild by leopard carpeting that also covered the built-in banquettes and X-form stool. In addition to the television, a turntable and speaker were also recessed into the wall—a rare concession by Madeleine to contemporary life.

At the same time as the Boulevard Suchet project, Mme Irène Liévoux, a longstanding client of the rue Jacob store, purchased the Neoclassical Château de Vauboyen sited slightly to the south of Paris. Decades before, in 1940, Madeleine had come across the chateau when Lèves was momentarily out of her hands and unsuccessfully offered its owner whatever he might want for it. It must have seemed written in the heavens when in 1974, her client purchased and decorated it, with her advice, in *le style* Castaing. Liévoux was well versed in the high-priestess' ways: she had frequented the shop for years and the two had even been on buying excursions together to England.

For Liévoux, the blue and green Castaing palette deeply resonated with her, and she found it reminded her of her native Russia. The blues evoked the dome of the church in the Russian cemetery of Sainte Geneviève-des-Bois in l'Essone and the greens reminded her of the malachite in St. Petersburg's Hermitage. Russian antique furniture completed the transformation of the chateau into her "Petit Pavlovsk." The dining room was where Madeleine and Liévoux collaborated most closely. The eau-de-nil walls and Indian silk curtains lined in the same green evoke a winter garden further enhanced by the floral and fauna carpeting. Nineteenth-century accoutrements, such as the tole floral chandelier wrapped with "make-believe" (i.e. plastic) green leaves, the pink and white scallop shell porcelain service, and even the design of the curtains which Liévoux modeled after period watercolors set the Tolstoian mood.

A la russe was also the mood for the Paris apartment of society hairdresser Alexandre Zouari. Madeleine's Russian red is the dominant note in the salon/dining room, and just as with the bedroom of the teenage Carole Weisweiller and the bachelor Raffaello von Banfield, she trimmed it with "Le Chale." The richness and warmth of the red supported by the opulent velvet textiles created a luxurious cushioned sanctum far away from the shrill and hectic demands of the modern world.

Madeleine paired the blue of the sky and green of the grass to meld the outside with indoors in the salon-library.

For the ultimate boundary blurring, the floral-and-foliage patterned carpet was also used to upholster the Napoleon III borne. This Paris residence was published in 1975, when Madeleine was already in her eighties.

Blue-and-white silk hangings trimmed with a border inspired by a Pompeian frieze projected Neoclassical refinement in the bedroom; Opposite: The densely patterned floral walls and the continuation of the "Carrelage Castaing" carpet into the hallway expanded the intimately scaled dining room.

Following: Orange walls and the appearance of a television set this room apart from any other in the Castaing canon. Madeleine mitigated the twentieth-century intrusion by recessing the entertainment equipment.

Irène Liévoux was one of Madeleine's faithful when she purchased the Neoclassical Château de Vauboyen. While many of the furnishings came from Madeleine and indeed *l'esprit* Castaing permeates all of the rooms, it was primarily the dining room that benefited directly from her touch.

The disciple learned from the high priestess well. From the bobble-fringe trimmed muslin to the unmistakable "coolie" lampshades from Bouchardeau, Mme Liévoux's bedroom is classic Castaing.

Furnished with a mix of nineteenth-century styles from Regency to Restoration, all of Madeleine's rooms are far away from the twentieth century.

Even if there appeared to be a codification of the Castaing look, with the similarities between the Zouari, Weissweiler, and von Banfield projects as just one example, Madeleine approached each one individually:

> I set up a house as a reflection of the person who will one day bring it to life. I come to know the master or mistress of the place. I find out what their thoughts are, what they read, who their company is. I make the décor according to who's going to live there. I rebel against the ordinary, cold, and impersonal formula of the standard apartment. I try to go against the mass-produced, even if it's a luxury item. When I've studied my client well, who in the meantime has become my friend, when I've made her talk, when I've heard her confession, I pride myself in creating the ambience that suits her disposition. I don't content myself with emphasizing a personality; I reveal it to her in a way.[16]

No matter how often themes are varied or repeated in *le style* Castaing—in many ways, this distinct look was one of her greatest secrets of success—each room was full of mystery, magic, and life.

Madeleine once said that the greatest achievement of her life was her and Marcellin's enduring love, but there is no doubt that she also found tremendous fulfillment in her career:

> I get the greatest satisfaction when I succeed, by putting him [my client] in an appropriate setting, in revealing my client to himself. Some of them actually swear to me that thanks to me, they feel happier, that in their whole lives and in what they do, they notice the beneficial effects of the new setting I designed for them.[17]

Madeleine was a master at layering patterns and passementerie as seen on this tabouret (opposite) and in this table setting (above) of *macarons* and majolica on a "Dentelle" moiré tablecloth, in client Mme Amar's residence; Following: Far from the formal settings usually characteristic of boiserie paneled rooms, the Amar salon is transported into a fairy woodland thanks to the floral "Duc de Morny" carpet and forest green velvet upholstery.

Preceding spread: Spaces for dining, reading, writing, and conversation were effortlessly incorporated into the large room; Above and opposite: Madeleine enrobed the salon of hairdresser Alexandre Zouari's apartment in a warm full-bodied red.

Following: Zouari's collection of Russian works of art were complemented by Madeleine's mélange of periods and provenance.

Madeleine Castaing died on December 18, 1992, just one day before her ninety-eighth birthday. For almost a century, she dedicated herself fully and confidently to her great loves: her husband, Marcellin, and the art of creating "maisons miroirs" for herself and for her clients. Lèves, her master-piece, was faithfully preserved by her son, Michel, until his death in 2004.

The Paris boutique, downsized to 30, rue Jacob, continued to operate under the direction of her devoted associate Laure Lombardini. The original space on the corner of the rues Bonaparte and Jacob was eventually taken over by the renowned tearoom Ladurée. Designer Roxane Rodriguez was contracted to decorate the space in the spirit of *le style* Castaing. Lombardini, who commented on how many imitated Mme Castaing but few failed to capture her touch, has yet to set foot there.

After Michel's death, the remaining inventory of the shop and storerooms, along with the contents of Lèves, were sent to Sotheby's, which, in conjunction with Galerie Charpentier, held a two-day single-owner sale on September 30 and October 1, 2004, in Paris. A pair of console tables, from the *salon de la rotonde*, brought the top bid, selling for over seven times their high estimate, as did many of the 729 items on offer. Were they worth it? "Ask the tables," Madeleine would have undoubt-edly said, knowing that, imbued as they were with the Castaing magic, they were beyond price.

Madeleine's grandson, Frédéric, has kept 30, rue Jacob for his autograph gallery. Its walls are painted a verdigris shade reminiscent of his grandmother's famous hue, but as he points out, it is more green and calls it "Frédéric Castaing blue."

While scouting locations for the 1996 film *The Proprietor*, Ismail Merchant of Merchant-Ivory Productions, came across Madeleine's rue Bonaparte apartment, which was, recalled Merchant, "the way it was left when Mme Castaing died, as if guests were expected for dinner." In the film, the apartment was used as the setting for another grande dame, Jeanne Moreau, who plays a revered expatriate novelist who is haunted by memories of her past. When she learns her childhood home in Paris is for sale, she sells everything so that she can buy it and, in owning and inhabiting it, come to terms with her past. It is no wonder that Madeleine's dreamy, out-of-time decoration was seized upon. Soon after filming, Merchant and his partner, James Ivory, purchased the apartment along with a select few items, including the white and black ceramic stove, from its original furnishings. Photographs from the period document the benignly neglected state of the apartment: The batting that covered the walls of the dining room and game room had become blackened with time, the plasterwork deteriorated, and Mr. Ivory remembers having to wear shoes in the bedroom on account of the soiled carpeting.

While her own artfully crafted personal settings have been dismantled and disbursed, *le style* Castaing lives on and continues to enchant. Although Maison Hamot closed in 1999, her signature fabrics and carpets are still in production, from which she made most of her money, according to some, as she never wanted to part with anything else in her shop. Edmond Petit offers a version edited by Bruno de Caumont of her line of fabrics, and Codimat continues to reproduce her carpets with plans to include more patterns from their Castaing archives in the near future.

As a new generation discovers the enchanted realm of Madeleine Castaing, there is no doubt that the cult of Castaing lives on and her spell remains unbroken.

APPENDIX: FABRICS AND CARPETS

Madeleine Castaing's world fearlessly and passionately embraced color and pattern. She took no heed of trends or conventions, and, in the pleasing of her own eye, attracted legions of admirers and imitators from all over the world.

If she was an aesthete par excellence, she was also a canny businesswoman: Within a few years of opening her shop during the German occupation of France, she had collaborated with the historic house of Hamot, established in 1762, to develop fabric and carpet designs that were sold under the Castaing imprimatur, and by so doing, created an instantly recognizable look. A brand was born.

Castaing derived most of her designs from document textiles, spanning the whole of the nineteenth century, from "Carrelage Castaing," a graphic Empire-style design featuring repeating rosettes, to "Duc de Morny," which is wildly splashed with flowers and cartouches and named after Napoleon III's half-brother. The archives of Maison Hamot were plumbed, and on several occasions, she simply used one of their existing designs, like "Feuillage Sylvie" or "Paiva," which graced the floor of her Paris entresol bedroom. The flea market was always a rich source for antique remnants, and photographs of her boutique reveal piles of vintage prints and woolens.

Perhaps more important than establishing a signature Castaing look, these lines also contributed significantly to her business's bottom line, and continue to do so: Nearly twenty years after her death, most of her designs are still in production. After Maison Hamot closed in 1999, Edmond Petit acquired the rights to the Castaing fabrics, with Clarence House as the United States stockist. With the help of designer Bruno de Caumont, many were reissued. Several designs were reinterpreted, such as "Bordure Pompeii," which became the repeating stripe "Lola Montez," or created in new colorways or materials. After initially working with Maison Hamot to realize her carpets, Madeleine soon went directly to Codimat, whose factory Catry carried out orders for both Hamot and Codimat. Codimat, who maintains it original premises on the rue du Cherche-Midi nearly adjacent to Madeleine's first shop, continues to weave the cut-pile wool carpets in Castaing designs.

And, so, a new generation, charmed and captivated by *le style* Castaing, is able to inject a little of it into their own *maisons miroirs*.

"Carrelage Castaing" carpet in off-white and black and "Percale Medallion" in pink, sky blue, and white on the walls, curtain borders, and chair back are boldly paired in the young Carole Weisweiller's dressing room.

RAYURE CASTIGLIONE

BORDURE 11703*

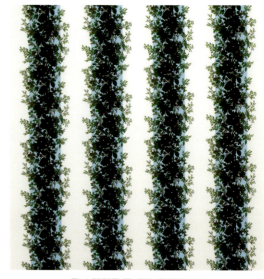

RAYURE FLEURIE

MACMAHON VERT

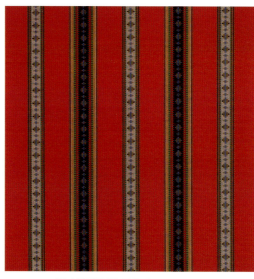

RAYURE BRODERIE

DENTELLE
(in percale and moiré)

RAYURE CACHEMIRE

LES LILAS*

BORDURE POMPEII
(reedited by Edmond Petit as "Lola Montes")

LOUISIANNE

GALATA

VOLUBILIS*

BAGATELLE

(very similar to "Rayure Fleurie"; reissued by Edmond Petit from archival
Madeleine Castaing fabric at the request of designer Jean-Paul Beaujard)

BRANCHES DE PIN

ETAMINE RAYÉE*

LES CAPUCINES*

(used by Bernard Castaing)

STAEL

PERCALE MEDALLION*

* NO LONGER IN PRODUCTION

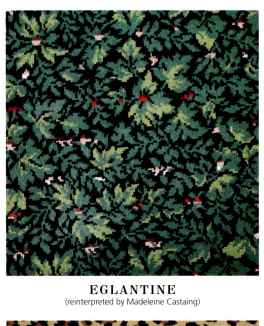

EGLANTINE
(reinterpreted by Madeleine Castaing)

PATTERSON*
(used by Madeleine Castaing)

FEUILLES DE BANANIER

LÉOPARD MADELEINE CASTAING

FEUILLAGE SYLVIE*
(Hamot archives; used by Madeleine Castaing)

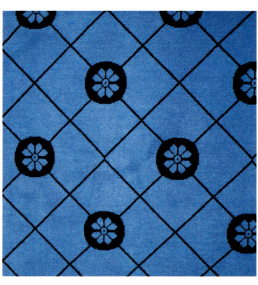

CARRELAGE CASTAING sans ANCRE
(adaptation by Bernard Castaing)

CHARLES X PERLÉ*
(reinterpreted by Madeleine Castaing)

VAUBAN MADELEINE CASTAING

PAIVA
(Hamot archives; used by Madeleine Castaing)

PANTHÈRE MADELEINE CASTAING

CACHEMIRE MADELEINE CASTAING
(in green and black)

DUC DE MORNY*

VAUBAN MADELEINE CASTAING

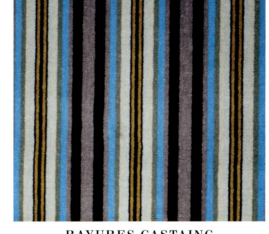

RAYURES CASTAING

CARRELAGE CASTAING

FEUILLES DE LIERRE
(used by Madeleine Castaing)

MOIRÉ
(used by Madeleine Castaing)

LYNX MADELEINE CASTAING

✴ NO LONGER IN PRODUCTION

NOTES

IN SEARCH OF LOST TIME

1. Quoted in *Madeleine Castaing*, a documentary by David Rocksavage, 52 minutes, broadcast by France 3, INA France, June 4, 1986.
2. Marie-France Boyer, "Diva of the rue Jacob," *World of Interiors* (May 1986): 88.
3. François-Marie Banier, "Madeleine Castaing entre le peintre et Proust," *Le Monde*, July 29, 1982, 13.
4. "La petite Madeleine des décorateurs," *Maison française* (September 1987): 99.
5. Jean-Noël Liaut, *Madeleine Castaing* (Paris: Payot, 2008), 19–20.
6. The convent's order was *Les Dames Blanches not Les Visitadines*. Jean-Louis de Rambures, "L'étrange bonne dame de la rue Jacob," *Réalités* (January 1963): 64–69.
7. Quoted in Rocksavage.
8. Liaut, 30.
9. Boyer, 86.
10. Liaut, 31, as recounted by Carlo Jansiti.
11. Quoted in Rocksavage.
12. "Le heures chaudes de Montparnasse, À la recherche de Chaim Soutine," broadcast on France 2 INA, December 20, 1986.
13. Catherin Fisher, "The Secret of Soutine: An Interview with Madeleine Castaing," *Apollo* (February 1992): 94.
14. Maurice Sachs, *Le Sabbat* (Paris: Gallimard, 1960), 84–85.
15. Suzanne Sens, *Découverte d'Erik Satie* (Maulévrier, Maine-et-Loire: Herault, 1984): 107–10.
16. As cited by Liaut, 56.
17. "Le bal du siècle," broadcast by France 5, August 2006.
18. Liaut, 69.
19. Again, different versions abound of this story. One is that Carco agreed to trade it for a Derain and another is that Carco had been given the painting by Zborowski a few months earlier. Carco gave back the painting to Zborowski and refused any payment for the work. Dan Franck, *Bohemian Paris: Picasso, Modigliani, Matisse, and the Birth of Modern Art* (New York: Grove Press, 2001), 372.
20. Edme Restif, "Un dimanche a Lèves," *La Depeche d'Eure-et-Loir*, August 23, 1934.
21. Rocksavage.
22. Fisher, 96.
23. Waldemar George, *L'Atelier d'Art* (May–June 1939): 15–16.
24. Fisher, 96.
25. Fisher, 98.
26. Rachel Stella and John Yau, "Madeleine Castaing Reminisces about Chaim Soutine," *Arts Magazine* (December 1984): 71–73.
27. Fisher, 97.

LÈVES

1. Madeleine Castaing quoted in Jean-Louis de Rambures, "L'étrange bonne dame de la rue Jacob," *Réalités* (January 1963): 66.
2. Maurice Sachs, *Le Sabbat* (Paris: Gallimard, 1960), 369.
3. Madeleine quoted in *Madeleine Castaing*, a documentary by David Rocksavage, 52 minutes, broadcast by France 3, INA France, June 4, 1986.
4. Madeleine quoted in Rocksavage.
5. The facade was first painted ochre, and then green before she struck upon the blue.
6. Astrid Guillon, *Madeleine Castaing (1894–1992)*, (unpublished thesis, University of Paris, Sorbonne-Pantheon, 2006), 69.
7. Christopher Petkanas, "Historic Houses: Madeleine Castaing at Lèves," *Architectural Digest* (July 1995): 78
8. Sachs, 370.
9. Louise de Vilmorin, *Madame de suivi de Julietta* (Paris: Gallimard, 1951), 234.
10. Honoré de Balzac, trans. James Waring, *The Lily of the Valley* (London: Dent, 1800s), 51.
11. Jean-Noël Liaut, *Madeleine Castaing* (Paris: Payot, 2008), 31. According to Josette Castaing, Madeleine's daughter-in-law married to Michel.
12. de Rambures, 64.
13. Liaut, 151.
14. Madeleine quoted in de Rambures, 66.
15. de Rambures, 68.
16. The same chintz was used, among others, for clients Nina Ricci, Jean Voilier, and Francine Weisweiller.
17. Honoré de Balzac, trans. Charlotte Mandell, *The Girl with the Golden Eyes* (New York: Melville House, 2007), 85. He wrote: "This boudoir was hung with a red fabric overlaid by the sheerest Indian chiffon, fluted like a Corinthian column, its folds alternately hollow and full, ending at both top and bottom in a poppy red band of cloth on which black arabesques were outlined. Beneath the sheer muslin, the red cloth showed as pink, an amorous color that was repeated by the curtains on the window, made of Indian chiffon lined with pink taffeta."
18. Ibid., 86.
19. de Rambures, 66.
20. François-Marie Banier, "Madeleine Castaing entre le peintre et Proust," *Le Monde*, July 29, 1982, 11.

ACT TWO: MADELEINE THE MERCHANT

1. Louise de Vilmorin, *Madame de suivi de Julietta* (Paris: Gallimard, 1951), 184.
2. Alexandra D'Arnoux, "Le style Castaing: Un art de vivre," *Elle Décoration* (March 1990): 112.
3. *Madeleine Castaing*, a documentary by David Rocksavage, 52 minutes, broadcast by France 3, INA France, June 4, 1986.
4. Author's interview with Frédéric Castaing and Laure Lombardini, May 2009.
5. Jean-Noël Liaut, *Madeleine Castaing* (Paris: Payot, 2008), 116–17. The author is indebted to Liaut's research as his biography is the only account of her having opened a stall before her shop as well as placing the date of 1941 for the opening of the rue du Cherche-Midi boutique.
6. Napoleon's laundress, Cathérine Hübscher, whose husband was elevated to the rank of duke by the emperor. Her uncouthness and vulgar language at court gave rise to her nickname.
7. Rocksavage.
8. Jean-Louis de Rambures, "L'étrange bonne dame de la rue Jacob," *Réalités* (January 1963): 66.
9. Christopher Petkanas, "Historic Houses: Madeleine Castaing at Lèves," *Architectural Digest* (July 1995): 82.
10. Émile Zola, trans. Douglas Parmee, *Nana* (London: Penguin, 1972), 336.
11. de Rambures, 68.
12. *Chroniques de France*, "Madeleine Castaing," with Jean-Noël Roy, magazine #39, 1970, BNF.
13. According to François-Marie Banier in Christopher Flach, *Madeleine Castaing*, documentary.
14. Alexandra D'Arnoux, "Le Style Castaing: un art de vivre," *Elle Décoration* (March 1990): 112
15. D'Arnoux, 112.
16. Alec Weisweiller, as cited by his daughter from May 2009 author's interview with Carole Weisweiller.
17. Katie Archer interview with Roland Seigneur, February 4, 2010.
18. Rocksavage.
19. Marie-France Boyer, "Diva of the rue Jacob," *World of Interiors* (May 1986): 83
20. Also referred to as "Rayure Hongroise," and in the United States as "Rayure Madeleine."
21. Marie-France Boyer, "Diva of the rue Jacob," *World of Interiors* (May 1986): 92. The full quote from Madeleine: "I don't care for 'eastern' carpets, or rather I don't like exoticism, I'm not much of a traveler."
22. "Madeleine Castaing, la décoration, une histoire d'amour," *Maison et jardin* (October 1987): 45.
23. Due to safety regulations, the papers are no longer coated with a toxic hardener, which has changed the color of blue. According to Madeleine Cateron, the current owner of Abat Jour Bouchardeau, the firm was very integral to the Castaing shades of green, rose, and her signature blue. The Bouchardeaus's suppliers provided a variety of color samples from which Mme Castaing selected. Author interview with Madeleine Cateron by Elizabeth Tenney, September 4, 2009.
24. de Rambures, 69.
25. Rocksavage.
26. de Rambures, 67.
27. Rockavage.
28. As cited by Liaut, 148.
29. As cited by Liaut, 149.
30. Carol Vogel, "Romantic Gestures in Paris, NYC," *The New York Times Style Magazine*, November 23, 1986, 118.
31. Laure Lombardini as cited by Liaut, 173.

LE STYLE MALMAISON

1. In *Madeleine Castaing*, a documentary by David Rocksavage, 52 minutes, broadcast by France 3, INA France, June 4, 1986.
2. Thomas Kernan, ed., *Les Nouvelles Réussites de la décoration française* (Paris: Condé Nast, 1960), 7.
3. Thomas Kernan, ed., *The Finest Rooms in France* (New York: Viking, 1967), 8. First published in France in 1960 as *Les Nouvelles Réussites de la décoration française.*
4. It is important to remember that style didn't change the minute a ruler vacated a throne, hence labeling styles by ruler is to a degree arbitrary. I adopt it for this, because in France, there was a more direct relationship to reign and corresponding style and for the reason that these labels have a general acceptance and understanding.
5. Stephen Calloway, *Twentieth-Century Decoration* (New York: Rizzoli, 1988), 305.
6. Marquise de la Tour du Pin, trans. and ed. Walter Geer, *Recollections*, (New York: Brentano's, 1920), 311.
7. Eleanor DeLorme, ed., *Joséphine and the Arts of the Empire* (Los Angeles: Getty Publications, 2005), 67.
8. *The Finest Rooms in France*, 309–11.
9. "Le Style Directoire," *Connaissance des arts* (July 1956): 33.
10. "A propos des nouveaux aménagements du château de Malmaison," *Connaissance des arts* (July 1955): 59. "Non seulement ces bougies donnent plus d'élégance aux luminaires, mais elles confèrent à toutes les pièces l'impression d'être prêtes pour une réception."
11. Marie-France Boyer, "Diva of the rue Jacob," *World of Interiors* (May 1986): 92.
12. Eveline Schlumberger, "En homage à Gérard Mille," *Connaissance des arts* (April 1964): 66.
13. Christopher Flach, *Madeleine Castaing*, documentary, 2008.
14. Mrs. Raymond Guest was the Princess Caroline Murat who was descended from Napoleon's chief of cavalry who in turn was married to Napoleon's youngest sister, Caroline.
15. Francis Spar, ed., *Le Style Anglais, 1750–1850* (Paris: Librairie Hachette, 1959), 198.
16. Ibid., 195.
17. *Le Figaro*, April 1, 1986. Jean-Noël Liaut, *Madeleine Castaing* (Paris: Payot, 2008), 134.
18. Liaut, 134.
19. *Le Style anglais*, 7.
20. Ibid., 195.

A UNIVERSE "COCTEAU CASTAING"

1. Jean Cocteau, "Décor d'une jeune fille," *Connaissance des arts* (June 1961): 66.
2. Only a few years later, Guérin would have nothing to do with Cocteau or any of his friends who were also friends with Cocteau. The poet had introduced Guérin's younger brother Jean to opium to which he became addicted.
3. Carole Weisweiller, *Je l'appelais Monsieur Cocteau* (Monaco: Éditions du Rocher, 2003), 24.
4. Ibid., 24–25.
5. Cocteau's account of "tattooing" the villa's walls from the documentary *La villa Santo-Sospir* (1952): "When I stayed at Santo Sospir in the summer of 1950 I hastily decorated a wall. Matisse told me that if you decorate one wall you should do the others as well. He was right. Picasso opened and closed all the doors. All that was left was to paint the doors. That is what I tried to do.

"But the doors lead into rooms. The rooms have walls. And if the doors are painted the walls have an empty look. I spent the entire summer of 1950 working on ladders. An old Italian worker prepared my pigments, immersed in fresh milk. A young woman lives at Santo Sospir. I didn't need to dress the walls. I had to draw on their surface. That's why I made line frescoes, with a few colors that echo tattoo art. Santo Sospir is a tattooed villa."
6. Jean-Louis Gaillemin, "Historic Houses: Jean Cocteau at Cap-Ferrat," *Architectural Digest* (July 1983): 140.
7. Picasso came to watch the filming and did a sketch of Francine in the dress that she kept in her bedroom. Gaillemin, 143.
8. Ibid., 139.
9. Weisweiller, 100.
10. Ibid., 111.
11. Jean Cocteau, "Décor d'une jeune fille," *Connaissance des arts* (June 1961): 66.
12. Weisweiller, 117.
13. Gaillemin, 140.
14. Cocteau, 66.

OF MAISONS MIROIRS

1. "Madeleine Castaing, la décoration, une histoire d'amour," *Maison et jardin* (October 1987): 45.
2. Jean-Noël Roy, "Madeleine Castaing," *Chroniques de France* series, 1970, BNF, cited by Astrid Guillon, *Madeleine Castaing (1894–1992)*, unpublished thesis, Paris, 2006.
3. Katie Archer interview with Roland Seigneur, February 4, 2010.
4. Jean-Louis de Rambures, "L'étrange bonne dame de la rue Jacob," *Réalités* (January 1963): 68–69.
5. *Madeleine Castaing*, a documentary by David Rocksavage, 52 minutes, broadcast by France 3, INA France, June 4, 1986.
6., "La Résidence française, exposition organisée par Art et Industrie," *Art et industrie* no. VIII (1947): 16.
7. Christie's London included the following note in the lot description of a watercolor of Mme "Ferenzi's" (many different spellings of the client's last name abound) dining room by Alexander Serebriakoff: "This is thought to be the first flat to be decorated in 'le goût anglais' in postwar Paris by Madelaine Castaing." Christie's London, *Interiors Watercolours*, November 17,1994, lot 160.
8. Les Abat-Jour de Bouchardeau was founded by Monsieur and Madame Bouchardeau together in 1936, first at a location on rue de La Cerisaie, moving it to its current location on 13, rue de L'Arsenal shortly thereafter in 1939. Madeleine would usually have Laure Lombardini phone in the measurements she wanted for a new lampshade. No drawings were necessary as the measurements of the top and bottom were enough to create a model for the lampshade. Madeleine never came to the Bourchardeau atelier as she already had special lampshade models already made in a drawer to refer to when placing orders. The Bouchardeaus, and later on Cateron and her new assistant (who is now the current owner) went to Madeleine's store to show off the lampshades and drop off the final products. They never went directly to the clients' homes or apartments for the installation of their lamps as this would have created direct competition with Madeleine. Bouchardeau also wired the lamps for electricity when necessary. Elizabeth Tenney interview with Madeleine Cateron, September 4, 2009.
9. Archer. Seigneur opened in 1935 at 6, rue des Quatre-vents where it is still located.
10. Located in a new modern building, the apartment most likely was a naked box.
11. Jean-Noël Liaut, *Madeleine Castaing* (Paris: Payot, 2008), 178
12. Hélène Cingria, "Sous le signe de la mode at de la fantaisie," *Art et Décoration* (April 1961): 40–43.
13. Rocksavage.
14. To Banier in Rocksavage.
15. Archer.
16. "La Résidence française," 41.
17. de Rambures, 69.

BIBLIOGRAPHY

Aillaud, Charlotte. "Country Life in Paris: Carole Weisweiller's Retreat on the Right Bank." *Architectural Digest* (February 1991): 194–97, 206.

D'Arnoux, Alexandra. "Le Style Castaing: un art de vivre." *Elle Décoration* (March 1990): 102–12.

Banier, François-Marie. "Madeleine Castaing entre le peintre et Proust." *Le Monde*, July 29, 1982, 11, 13.

Barotte, René. "Soutine." *Plaisir de France*, May 1973, 42–49.

Boyer, Marie-France. "Château de Vauboyen." *World of Interiors* (March 1985): 78–91.

——————. "Diva of the rue Jacob." *World of Interiors* (May 1986): 80–93.

Briest, Francis. *L'aigle et sa légende* Auction. (Paris). November 19, 1997.

Brubach, Holly. "With an eye for the unconventional, Madeleine Castaing transformed French taste." *House and Garden* (July 1993): 20–23.

Castaing, Marcellin, and Jean Leymarie. *Soutine.* Paris/Lausanne: La Bibliothèque des Arts, 1963.

"Un certain chintz." *Maison et Jardin* (November 1959): 102–03.

Chery, Christian. "Romantisme bien pensé." *Art et Décoration* (October 1962): 10–15.

Ch., B. "Le XIXe siècle et la sobriété des lignea." *Art et Décoration* no. 12 (1949): 22–24.

Cingria, Hélène. "Sous le signe de la mode at de la fantaisie." *Art et Décoration* (April 1961): 40–43.

Cocteau, Jean. "Décor d'une jeune fille." *Connaissance des art* (June 1961): 66–71.

"Comment décore-t-on a Paris?" *Maison et jardin* (December 1956–Jan 1957): 126–29.

"Une décoratrice parisienne installe sa propre demeure." *Connaissance des arts* (November 1953): 32–37.

"Décors de la vie salon Madeleine Castaing." *Art et Industrie*, no. VI (1947): 16–21.

DeLorme, Eleanor, ed. *Joséphine and the Arts of the Empire.* Los Angeles: Getty Publications, 2005.

Depland, Daniel. *Mes putains sacrées.* Paris: Grasset, 2004.

"Exotisme a l'anglaise dans un jardin d'Auteuil." *Maison et jardin* (November 1955): 72–73.

Fisher, Catherin. "The Secret of Soutine: An Interview with Madeleine Castaing." *Apollo* (February 1992): 94–98.

Gaillard, Annick. "Chez Francine Weisweiller." *Jour de France*, January 15, 1966, 56–57.

Gaillemin, Jean-Louis. "Historic Houses: Jean Cocteau at Cap-Ferrat." *Architectural Digest* (July 1983): 139–44.

Giovannini, Joseph. "Ismail Merchant: The Producer-director Takes on Madeleine Castaing's Paris Apartment." *Architectural Digest* (April 1996): 178–85.

Gontaut-Biron, Chita de. "Madeleine Castaing nous ouvre les portes de sa thébaïde." *Connaissance des Arts* (November 1979): 96–101.

Guillon, Astrid. *Madeleine Castaing (1894–1992),* unpublished thesis, University of Paris, Sorbonne-Pantheon, 2006.

Hamel, Bruno de. "Historic Houses: Memories of Jean Cocteau; the Poet's Presence Strongly Felt at Milly-la-Forêt." *Architectural Digest* (October 1980): 150–55.

Hampton, Mark. *Legendary Decorators of the Twentieth Century.* New York: Doubleday, 1992, 245–51.

Joubeaux, Hervé, and Pierre Falicon. *Le temps retrouvé chez Madeleine Castaing: Photographies de Claire Flanders.* Chartres: Musée des Beaux-Arts, 1997.

Kernan, Thomas, ed. *The Finest Rooms in France.* New York: Viking, 1967.

——————. *Les Nouvelles Réussites de la decoration française, 1950–1960.* Paris: Éditions du Pont Royal, 1960.

Kochno, Boris. *Christian Bérard.* London: Thames and Hudson, 1988.

Lawford, Valentine. "Madame Castaing chez elle." *Architectural Digest* (September 1977): 130–37.

Liaut, Jean-Noël. *Madeleine Castaing: Mécène à Montparnasse Décoratrice à Saint-Germain-des-Près.* Paris: Payot, 2008.

Lovatt-Smith, Lisa. *Paris Interiors = Intérieurs Parisiens.* Cologne: Taschen, 1994.

Owens, Mitchell. "A legendary shop shuffles off to a new home." *The New York Times*, April 6, 2000, F3.

Peppiatt, Michael. "Jacques Grange: Spaces that resonate with the echoes of Emilio Terry and Madeleine Castaing." *Architectural Digest* (January 2001): 158–63, 210.

Petkanas, Christopher. "Historic Houses: Madeleine Castaing at Lèves." *Architectural Digest* (July 1995): 78–85.

"La petite Madeleine des décorateurs." *Maison Française* (September 1987): 96–105.

"Petits ou grand, les enfants veulent 'leur' chambre." *Connaissance des arts* (September 1958): 69.

Plas, Solange de. "Variations sur le XIXe siècle." *Art et Décoration* (July/August 1975): 48–51.

"Pour ou par un académicien." *Maison et jardin* (February 1956): 70–75.

Rambures, Jean-Louis de. "L'étrange bonne dame de la rue Jacob." *Réalités* (January 1963): 64–69.

Remilleux, Jean-Louis. *Groussay.* Paris: Albin Michel, 2007.

"La Résidence Française, exposition organisée par Art et Industrie." *Art et Industrie* no. VIII (1947): 13–24.

Restif, Edme. "Un dimanche a Lèves." *La Depeche d'Eure-et-Loir*, August 23, 1934.

Sachs, Maurice. *Lettres.* Paris: Le Bélier, 1968.

——————. *Le Sabbat.* Paris: Gallimard, 1960.

Schlumberger, Eveline. "L'objet extraordinaire: la maison de Mme Alec Weisweiller au Cap-Ferrat dont les murs sont 'tatoués' par Jean Cocteau." *Connaissance des arts* (October 15, 1956): 66–69.

"Six décors au goût du jour." *Connaissance des Arts* (September 1962): 58–63.

Slesin, Suzanne. "An antiques dealer's legendary style." *The New York Times Magazine,* October 16, 1986.

Sotheby's. *Impressionist and Modern Art.* London: Sotheby's, June 21, 2004.

Sotheby's, and Galerie Charpentier. *L'univers de Madeleine Castaing, mobilier et objets d'art de sa demeure de Lèves et de sa galerie rue Jacob.* Paris: Sotheby's, September 30 and October 1, 2004.

Spar, Francis, ed. *Le Style Anglais, 1750–1850.* Paris: Librairie Hachette, 1959.

Stella, Rachel, and John Yau. "Madeleine Castaing Reminisces about Chaim Soutine." *Arts Magazine* (December 1984): 71–73.

Stoeltie, Barbara, and René Stoeltie. *Adieu Lèves.* N.p, 2006.

——————. "Au revoir, Lèves." *The World of Interiors* (September 2004): 108–19.

——————. *Chez elles: le décor au féminin.* Paris: Flammarion, 2003.

De Vilmorin, Louise. *Madame de suivi de Julietta.* Paris: Gallimard, 1951.

Vogel, Carol. "Romantic Gestures in Paris, NYC." *The New York Times Style Magazine,* November 23, 1986, 115–19.

"La Vogue du style anglais." *Connaissance des Arts* (December 1952): 44–45.

"Voici les derières réalisations de la decoratrice la plus épiée a Paris." *Connaissance des arts* (July 1957): 22–25.

Weisweiller, Carole. *Je l'appelais Monsieur Cocteau.* Monaco: Éditions du Rocher, 2003.

AUDIO-VISUAL

"Le bal du siècle." Broadcast by France 5, August 2006.

Chroniques de France, "Madeleine Castaing." With Jean-Noel Roy. Magazine #39, 1970, BNF.

Flach, Christopher. *Madeleine Castaing.* Documentary, 34 minutes, 2008.

"Les heures chaudes de Montparnasse, la recherche de Chaim Soutine." Broadcast on France 2 INA France, December 20, 1986.

Rocksavage, David. *Madeleine Castaing.* Documentary, 52 minutes, broadcast by France 3, INA France, June 4, 1986.

INDEX

Adam, Robert, *153*
Amar, Mme, residence of, *250–53*
Amido, 106
Aragon, Louis, *Il ne m'est Paris que d'Elsa*, 24
Art Deco, 134
Art et industrie, 210, *211*

"Bagatelle" fabric pattern, *265*
Ballets Russes, 30
Balzac, Honoré de, 20, 21, *20–21*, 210
   La fille aux yeux d'or, 76, 125
   Le Lys dans la vallée, 16, , 46–47
Banfield, Raffaello de, apartment of, 222, *230–33*, 251
Banier, François-Marie, 98, *126–27*, 155
Barnes, Albert C., 35
Barroux, Jacques and Henri, 174, 183
Beistegui, Charles de, 134, 147, 150, *152, 158–59*
Belle et la bête, La (film), 168
Bérard, Christian "Bébé," 80, 160, *160, 162–63*, 168, *168–69*
Berthault, Louis-Martin, 142
Billiet, Joseph, 142
"Bordure 11703" fabric pattern, *264*
"Bordure Pompeii" fabric pattern, 263, *264*
Borghese, Pauline, chaises of, *145*
Bouchardeau firm, 97, 215, *249*, 268n8, 268n24
Boudin, Stéphane, *141*
Boudon, Joseph, 106
Boulevard Suchet apartment, 235, 240, *240–47*
"Branches de Pin" fabric pattern, *80–81, 265*
Braque, Georges, 27
Bresson, Robert, 168
Breteuil, Henri de, *22–23*
Brune, Pierre, 32
Burgues, Rodolphe, 13

"Cachemire Madeleine Castaing" carpet pattern, *82–83*, 222, *224–25, 267*
Calloway, Stephen, 134
Carco, Francis, 33
carpet patterns, *8–9*, 40, *50–51*, 55, *73–75, 80–83*, 92, *94, 95, 112–14, 132–33, 136–37, 182–83*, 222, *224–25, 240–45, 260–61, 262–63*
"Carrelage Castaing" carpet pattern, *8–9, 112–14, 132–33, 244–45, 262–63*, 263, *267*
"Carrelage Castaing sans Ancre" fabric pattern, *266*
Casarès, Maria, 168, *168–69*
Castaing, Bernard, 23, *76–77*
Castaing, Frédéric, *6–7*, 7, 79, 260
Castaing, Madeleine, *6–7*, *11–14, 16–17, 24–27, 30–31*, 36, *78–79*, 83, 106, *106–14, 160–61, 208–09*, 215, *232–35*, 263, *263*
   colors used by, 40, 76, *92–93*, 97, 268n24
   creation of distinctive look, 46–47
   death, 260
   as decorator, 208–59
   early life, 13, 16, 23
   flea markets frequented by, 51, 98, 101, *101–3*, 263
   hats of, *16–17, 78–79, 208–9*, 235
   later-life appearance, 235
   at Lèves, 39–40, *42*, 46–47, 51, 55, 76
   marché Jules-Vallès stand, 80
   marriage, 23, 76
   as merchant, 11, 79–80, 83, 88, 91–92, 97–98, 101, 106, 168, 173, 209
   move to Paris, 23–24, 27
   nickname, 51
   rue Bonaparte shop, *80–87*, 83, *145, 213*, 260
   rue Bonaparte upstairs apartment, *34–35*, 106, *114–33*, 125, *164*, 260
   store assistants of, 101, 106
   storerooms, 51, 80, 101, *104–5*, 168, 173
   Weisweiller commissions, 168
Castaing, Marcellin, 9, *12–13*, 16, *16–17*, 23, 24, 39, *76–77*, 79, *83*
   acquisition of Lèves, 39

death, 76, 106, 235
   marriage, 23, 76
Castaing, Michel, 23, *24–25, 30–31*, 40, *76–77*, 260
Castaing blue, 97, *221*
Castaings' art collecting, 27, 30, 32–33, 39–40, 79
Cateron, Madeleine, 268n8, 268n24
Caumont, Bruno de, 261, 263
Cendrars, Blaise (Sauser, Frédéric Louis), *26–27*, 30, 32
Chagall, Marc, 27
Chanel, Coco, 11, 235
"Charles X Perlé" carpet pattern, *266*
Chartres, 13, 16
Château de Breteuil, *22–23*
Château de Chenonceau, 150
Château de Compiègne (Josephine's house), *95*
Château de Groussay, 150, *152–53, 158–59*
Château de Rochecotte, 150
Château de Saché (Margonne's house), *20–21*
Château de Thuilerie, 222
Château de Vauboyen, 240, *248–49*
Chateaubriand, François-René de, 16, *18–19*
Cocteau, Jean, *166–67*
   Académie Française induction, 183, *185*
   benefactress of, 168, 173–74, 183
   Castaing's introduction to, 167–68
   Décor d'une jeune fille, 167
   La Difficulté d'étre, *196*
   films of, 168, 173, 183
   Milly-la-Forêt country house, 168, 183, *193–207*, 196
   in Montparnasse, 27, 30
   wall decoration of Santo-Sospir, 173, 196
Codimat firm, 261
Crucifix, Madame, 101
Cubism, 35

Dames du Bois de Boulogne, Les (film), 168, *168–69*
Damiot, Jacques, 80, 101
d'Ayen, Solange, 133
DeLorme, Eleanor, 137, 142
"Dentelle" fabric pattern, 92, *92–93, 132–33*, 251, *264*
Derain, André, 27
Dermit, Edouard, 173, *204*
Diaghilev, Serge, 30
Dino, duchesse de, 150
Dreyfus Affair, 13
"Duc de Morny" carpet pattern, 263, *267*
Dufy, Raoul, *198*

"Eglantine" carpet pattern, *73–75, 240–43, 266*
enfants terribles, Les (film), 168
English Regency style, 11, *59–61*, 116, *132–33, 140*, 142, 155, *156*, 160, *164–65, 172–73*, 210, *210–11, 214–15, 217*
"Etamine Rayée" fabric pattern, *265*
Exposition internationale des arts décoratifs et industriels modernes, 134

fabric patterns, 11, *54–55*, 55, *62, 80–81, 86*, 92, *92–93, 132–33*, 183, 240, *240–41, 260–61*, 263, *264–65*
Faure, Elie, 35
Fellous, Mireille, apartment of, *136–37, 220–21*
Ferenczi, Mme H., decorations for, 210, *214–15*, 215, *218–19*
"Feuillage Sylvie" carpet pattern, 263, *266*
"Feuilles de Bananier" carpet pattern, *182–83, 266*
"Feuilles de Lierre" carpet pattern, *158–59, 267*
Floréal, 24
Fontaine, François-Léonard, 137
Frank, Jean-Michel, 235

"Galata" fabric pattern, *265*
Gance, Abel, 32
Geffroy, Georges, 134, *134–35*
Glinshe, Paulette, 101
Gouel, Eva, 27
Grange, Jacques, *8–9*, 9, 101
Gray, Eileen, 106

Guérin, Jacques, 167
Guérin, Jean, 268n2
Guest, Mr. and Mrs. Raymond, residence of, *154–55*, 155
Guillaume, Paul, 80, 83
Guinness, Loel and Gloria, apartment of, *134–35*
Guiraud, Raoul, *140, 165*

Hagnauer, Jean-Philippe, *156*
Hagnauer antiquaire, 101, *171*
Hamot, François, 92, 97
Hübscher, Cathérine, 268n6

Iffla, Daniel Osiris, 142
Illiers-Combray, Proust's aunt's house in, *14–15*
Iribe, Paul, 142
Ivory, James, 260

J'accuse! (film), 32
Jacob family, 147
Jansen, 134, *141*, 155
Josephine, Empress, 40, *94–95*, 134, 137, 142, *144*, 147

Kernan, Thomas, 133
Khan, Aly, 210
Knoblock, Edward, 142

"La Résidence Française" showhouse, 210, *210–11*
La Rotonde café, Montparnasse, 27, *27–29*, 30, 32, 33
La Ruche (artists' colony), 33
la Tour du Pin, Mme de, 137
Labourdette, Elina, 168
L'aigle à deux têtes (film), 168, *168–69*, 183
Lancaster, Nancy, 76
Le Corbusier, 150
le style Castaing, 9, *10–11*, 46, 51, 76, 79, 80, 88, 91, 97, 106, 125, 155, 215, 251, 263
Ledoux, Claude-Nicolas, 147
Leduc, Violette, 210
Lefuel family, 147, *148–49*
Lenin, Vladimir, 27
"Léopard Madeleine Castaing" carpet pattern, *80–81, 94, 266*
leopard-patterned carpets and fabrics, *50–51*, 55, *95*, 97, *199–201, 245–47*
"Les Capucines" fabric pattern, *265*
"Les Lilas" fabric pattern, *264*
Lèves, *38–39*
   bathroom, *69*
   Castaing's acquisition of, 39
   Castaing's discovery of, 16
   Castaing's post-war reacquisition, 47
   dining room, *6–7*, 9, 55, *59–61*
   first-floor plan, *59*
   grounds, *30–31*, 40, *42–43*
   guest bedroom, *72–73*, 76
   hallway, 55, *64–65*
   Nymphaeum, 40, *43–45*
   Pink or Summer Bedroom, 55, *65–68*, 76, 222
   preservation of, 260
   salon de la rotonde, 40, *40–41, 48–58*, 51, 55, *145*, 260
   sitting room, *69–71*, 76
   Soutine at, 36, 39–40
   White or Winter Bedroom, 55, *62–63*
   World War II and, 47, 79
Liaut, Jean-Noël, 13, 33
Libion, Victor, 27
Liévoux, Irène, house of, 240, *248–49*
lighting, 40, *96–97*, 97
"Lola Montez" fabric pattern, 263, *264*
Lombardini, Laure, 16, *84–86*, 101, 210, 260, 268n8
Louis XIV, King of France, 134
"Louisianne" fabric pattern, *265*
"Lynx Madeleine Castaing" carpet pattern, *267*

MacMahon, Patrice de, 222
"MacMahon Vert" fabric pattern, *264*

Magistry, Auguste (father), 13
Magistry, Gérard (brother), 167
Magistry, Noëlie (mother), 13, 23
Magistry, Roger (brother), 23
Maison Hamot, 55, 92, 97, 215, 260, 263
Malmaison (Empress Josephine's house), 40, 125
    bedroom, *137–39*
    Council Room, *146–47*
    entrance hall, *142–43*
    redecoration of, 142, 147
Malmaison style, *132–65*
Malraux, André, 235
Marais, Jean, 168
    Cocteau's sculpture of, 196
    country house of, *170–71*
marché Jules-Vallès, Castaing's stand at, 80
Margonne, Jean de, *20–21*
Massine, Léonide, 30
Matisse, Henri, 27
Merchant, Ismail, 260
Mille, Gérard, 134, 147
Miller, Henry, 32
Milly-la-Forêt, Cocteau's country house, 168, 183, *193–207*, 196
Mitchell, Margaret, *Gone with the Wind*, 213
"Mme D," decorations for, 210, 215, *216*
Modigliani, Amedeo, 27, 33
"Moiré" carpet pattern, *267*
Moreau, Jeanne, 260
Morisot, Berthe, 173
Mortefontaine, Weisweiler's country house, 168, *172*, 173

Napoleon, Emperor of France, 137, 142
Napoleon III style, 11, 91, *100–101*, *117–19*, 210
Neoclassicism, *132–35*, 134, 137, 142, 147, 150, 155, *230*, *248–49*
Niarchos, Stavros, 150
Noailles, Charles and Marie-Laure de, 30, 150, *157*, 174

"Paiva" carpet pattern, 263, *266*
"Panthère Madeleine Castaing" carpet pattern, *267*
Parade ballet, 30, *178*
Paris
    post-World War I art scene, 24, 27, 30, 32–33, 35–36
    post-World War II conservatism, 133
    during World War II, 79–80
"Patterson" carpet pattern, *266*
Peck, Mrs., 210
"Percale Medallion," *265*
Percier, Charles, 137
Petit, Edmond, 261, 263
Picasso, Pablo, 27, 30, 268n7
Place des Etats-Unis *hôtel particulier* (Weisweiler residence), Paris, 168, 174, *180–87*, 183
Poiret, Paul, 142
de Poitiers, Diane, 150
Praz, Mario, 155, 160
Proprietor, The (film), 260
Proust, Marcel, 13, 46, 210
    À La Recherche du temps perdu, 23
    Aunt Leonie's house in Illiers-Combray, *14–15*
    Château de Breteuil and, *22–23*

Rainier III, Prince of Monaco, 150
"Rayure Broderie" fabric pattern, *54–55*, *92–93*, 264
"Rayure Cachemire" fabric pattern, 92, *92–93*, 183, *191*, 240, *240–41*, *250–51*, 264
"Rayure Castiglione" fabric pattern, *264*
"Rayure Fleurie" fabric pattern, 55, *62*, 92, *92–93*, *192*, 264, *265*
"Rayures Castaing" carpet pattern, *267*
Renoir, Pierre Auguste, *198*
Réussites de la décoration française, Les, *133–34*
Riccardi, Jean-Paul, 101, 106
Ricci, Nina, apartment of, 222, 235, *235–40*
Robain, Raymond, 47, 51
Rodriguez, Roxane, 260

roller blinds, hand-painted, *96–97*, 115
Rothschild, Nicole de, 168
Rouault, Georges, 30
Royal Pavilion, Brighton, *116*, 160, *164*
rue Bonaparte entresol apartment (Castaing residence), Paris, 106, *106–14*, *208–9*, 215, 263
rue Bonaparte shop, Paris, *80–87*, 83, *145*, *213*, 260
rue Bonaparte upstairs apartment (Castaing residence), Paris, *34–35*, 106, 125, 260
    bathroom, *126*
    bedroom, 125, *126–31*
    dining room, 106, *117–19*, *164*
    enfilade, 106, *122*, 125, *132–33*
    floor plan, *114*
    games room, *120–23*, 125
    grand salon, *124–25*
    hallways, 106, *115*, *116*
    kitchen, *117*
rue du Cherche-Midi storehouse (later shop), Paris, 51, 80, 101, 168, 173
rue La Bruyère *hôtel particulier* (Magistry residence), Paris, 13
rue Victorien-Sardou (Castaing residence), Paris, 24
rue Visconti storeroom, Paris, *104–5*
Ruhlmann, Emile-Jacques, 134

•

Sachs, Maurice, 30, 39, 46, 79, 167
Saint-Sauveur, Paul de, 106
Salon des Antiquaires, *159*, 235
Santo-Sospir, Weisweiler's villa, *166–67*, 168, 173–74, *174–79*, 196
Satie, Erik, 30, *30–31*, *178*
Seigneur, Roland, 91, 215
Serebriakoff, Alexandre, *158–59*, *216–17*
Simon, Simone, 168
Soane, John, 147
Sotheby's, 76, 260
Soutine, Chaim, *36*, *82–83*
    L'arbe de Vence, *59–61*
    Baigneuse, *34–35*
    Castaings as patrons of, 9, 35–36, 106
    Castaings' introduction to, 32–33
    death, 47
    Enfant de choeur, 35, *36–37*, 39
    La Femme au bain, *124–25*
    at Lèves, 36, 39–40, 47
    Le Pâtissier, 79
    portrait of Madeleine Castaing, *36–37*
    Une allée au printemps, 55
"Stael" fabric pattern, *265*
Stendhal, Maurice, 46
Süe, Louis, 134
Surrealism, 35, 150

Talleyrand, Charles-Maurice de, 150
tented rooms, 55, *62–63*, *136–37*, 137, 142, *192*, 210, *240–41*
Terry, Emilio, 134, 147, 150, *150–55*, 155, *157*, 159
Testament d'Orphée, Le (film), 173
Trotsky, Leon, 27

Utrillo, Maurice, 30

Vadim, Roger, 209
Vallé-aux-Loups (Chateaubriand's house), *18–19*
van Gogh, Vincent, 35
"Vauban Madeleine Castaing" carpet pattern, *266*, *267*
Verrières, Vilmorin's house in, 209–10
Villa des Roses (Saint-Prest), 13, 39, 46
Villa Santo-Sospir, La (film), 173, 268n5
Vilmorin, Louise de, 209–10
    Julietta, 13, 16, 46, 79
Voilier, Jean, house of, 222, *222–29*
"Volubilis" fabric pattern, *265*

Walter, Domenica, 80, 83
Weisweiler, Adam, 174

Weisweiler, Alec, 168, 173, 174
Weisweiler, Carole, 174
    Je l'appelais Monsieur Cocteau, 173
    residence, *188–89*, 210
    rooms of, 183, *190–93*, 240
Weisweiler, Francine, *180–81*, *186–87*
    as Cocteau's benefactress, 168, 173–74, 183, 196
    hôtel particulier residence, 168, 174, *180–87*, 183, *219*, 251
    Mortefontaine country house, 168, *172–73*, 173
    Santo-Sospir villa, *166–67*, 168, 173–74, *174–79*, 196
World War II, 47, 79, 133

Zborowski, Leopold, 33, 35
Zola, Émile, 46, 88
Zouari, Alexandre, apartment of, 240, 251, *254–59*
Zuber "Eldorado" panoramic wallpaper, *165*

ACKNOWLEDGMENTS

If entering the world of Madeleine Castaing felt a little like Alice stepping through the looking glass, there were many guides and sages to help me along the way. Frédéric Castaing and Mme Lombardini were inexhaustible in their patience and generosity, and I am indebted to them for letting me tell this story; Carole Weisweiller, Jacques Grange, Pierre Passebon, Roland Seigneur, Madeleine Cateron, and Jean-Paul Beaujard gave me many valuable insights; Pascal Pouliquen of Codimat and Charlotte Petit of Edmond Petit opened up their Castaing carpet and fabric archives, where I could have happily stayed forever. To James Ivory and Gil Donaldson, my deepest appreciation for opening the doors of Mme Castaing's former Paris apartment—an experience of time and place I will long hold close.

If my spoken French has degenerated over the years, a team of lovely ladies made sure I didn't miss a word: Liz Tenney, D'Arcy Flueck, and especially Katie Archer, whose lyrical translations grace these pages. Thank you to Enda Donaher, Laura Harvey, and Min Kim for their contributions.

This book owes everything to the incredibly talented photographers whose work is included herein, including Roland Beaufre and Jean-François Jaussaud, who captured with their lens the mystery and poetry of the Castaing universe. Sam Shahid and Betty Eng of Shahid and Company wove everything together with exquisite elegance. Thank you to Charles Miers at Rizzoli for believing an American could be entrusted with a French legend and to my editor Isabel Venero, for her constant encouragement.

My dear friend Beth Martell's effusive enthusiasm was always energizing and to her I owe my first introduction to Castaing style. Bernard, Barbara, and Rachel Karr were tremendously supportive throughout.

If there is one thing I have taken away from Madeleine's example is that rooms are for living and living is for loving, so to my husband Andrew, thank you for making ours full of life and love.

First published in the United States in 2010 by Rizzoli International Publications, Inc.
300 Park Avenue South, New York, NY 10010
www.rizzoliusa.com

Design by Sam Shahid

2010 2011 2012 2013 / 10 9 8 7 6 5 4 3 2 1

ISBN: 978-0-8478-3281-1

Library of Congress Control Number: 2010931999

PRINTED IN CHINA